Kent Lore

ALAN BIGNELL

Kent Lore

A Heritage of Fact and Fable

ROBERT HALE · LONDON

ISBN 0 7090 1013 3

Robert Hale Limited
Clerkenwell House
Clerkenwell Green
London EC1R 0HT

Photoset by Rowland Phototypesetting Ltd
Bury St Edmunds, Suffolk
Printed in Great Britain by
St Edmundsbury Press, Bury St Edmunds, Suffolk
Bound by Woolnough Bookbinders Ltd, Northants

Contents

Illustrations

All illustrations are reproduced courtesy of South Eastern Newspapers Limited.

1

The Lore Unto Itself

If the past is likened to a tapestry, the imagery could very well be extended so that history is the warp and lore the weft of the weave. The two are inseparable. Much of history is lore; much lore is history. Often, there is no certainty about which is which, or where one ends and the other takes up the tale.

But lore goes beyond history and seeps into areas in which history has no particular place at all. As well as the legends which have been passed down from one generation to another – perhaps losing, though sometimes, surely, gaining in definition over the years – lore embodies all sorts of life-enriching trivia. Old wives' tales, everyday expressions, beliefs and customs that add very little to history are the very stuff of lore. If they add little to the structure of life, they add enormously to its colour and interest.

Nor is lore always a relic of the past. Like history, it is always with us, emerging from the present like an irrepressible spring bubbling out of a rocky overgrowth in which nothing is very clear until it is looked back upon from a distance when the principal features thrust themselves upon the scene. The greater the distance from which it is viewed, the more clearly the stream sparkles and the more it compels the eye to take notice of it and return to it when it would stray away.

It would be perfectly possible to study history without giving any weight or acknowledgement to lore at all. Indeed, that has been done, and it is not, perhaps, too much to say that many a youthful curiosity about history has been nipped in the bud and turned to soured indifference by school textbooks compiled in just that way.

That is not to say that one should not be aware of the distinction between history and lore, and perhaps even more aware that it is not always at all clear just where that distinction starts. It is more to say that one should be most keenly aware of the interdependence of the two and not always try too hard to separate them out. They belong together, complementing each other, each giving the other a relevance it would lack alone.

Many years ago, when I first began to be interested in Kentish lore, I haunted the bookshops in search of books on the subject. I found a few. I had expected to find many more. I mentioned the dearth to a bookseller friend once.

'Kent doesn't have a lot of lore,' he suggested. 'I suppose it is because we have never been isolated from the mainstream of modernism in the way that other counties have. We have been too much trafficked by people coming and going, bringing the latest ideas from outside and taking our treatment of them here away with them.

'Kent has never been left alone long enough to gather the moss of lore.'

Well, there is certainly something in that. But I have come to the conclusion since that he was thinking of the fairly narrow concept of lore in which natural features of the countryside are attributed to fairies or giants or shadowy, semi-mythical heroes of the long past. In that sense, unlike, say Devon and Cornwall or the wilder parts of Yorkshire and Cumbria, it is true that Kent is comparatively lore-less.

We do not have any legends of fairies; no giants ever seem to have stalked our landscape. We are pretty short on legendary heroes, and there is no folk memory in this extreme south-east corner of the country of dragons or other mythical monsters (with the possible and very much tongue-in-cheek exception of the Folkestone Fiery Serpent, of which more later).

Our lore tends towards the much more prosaic kind; the kind that is firmly rooted in verifiable or demonstrable history. But of that we have no shortage at all. A great many of the stories in which Kentish history is told are concocted from a great deal of inherited lore (legend, if you prefer it) woven through an often pretty coarse canvas of indisputable fact.

Nor are we short of the kind of knowledge that tends to be passed on prefaced with the assurance that 'they do say . . .'. Even when time has invalidated the origins of some of these assertions, they persist and add their own splashes of colour to many a local scene.

Yet no writer ever mentions the villages of Murston, Teynham and Tonge, all near Sittingbourne on the North Kent coastal strip, without reviving the centuries-old saying: 'He that will not live long, Let him dwell at Murston, Teynham or Tonge.'

I have never come across any explanation for the couplet: 'Naughty Ashford, surly Wye, Poor Kennington hard by!' If ever there was a good reason for such a slander, it has been lost to memory, as far as I know, and I've certainly no reason at all to believe that it has any modern relevance of any kind.

A quite different kettle of fish is one of the best-known and certainly one of the most often-quoted Kentish rhymes:

> A Knight of Cales [Calais],
> A Gentleman of Wales,
> A Laird of the North Country;
> A Yeoman of Kent
> With his yearly rent
> Will buy them out, all three.

That states a truism of medieval Kent that survived in some measure into modern times, although the comparisons may not have been literally valid for centuries. It incidentally reveals a great deal about the origins of the Kentish character. Kent very early established a yeoman economy of small landowners, able to be independent in a way that tenant farmers in other parts of the country did not achieve until much later. The Kentish yeoman was not necessarily rich, but he was, to a much greater extent than many of his contemporaries elsewhere, his own man and was not to be easily made to do anything at all that he didn't want to do.

The yeomen farmers were a force in the land that their masters in rank could not ride roughshod over just whenever they pleased, but must carry their support along with them. That inevitably gave rise to a deep sense of stability and a sort of equality that, in some cases, manifests itself today in stubborn bloody-mindedness at any hint of imposition.

That independence was further nurtured by the county's geography. England does not approach any closer to the coast of France than Dover does to Calais. For centuries, Kent was the natural target of any would-be invader from the Continent of Europe – to some extent, even now, still is. It was, therefore, the main bulwark, the first line of defence against any invader with his sights set upon London, which for almost a thousand years has been the capital city and centre of national administration.

So it was very much in the self-interest of successive administrations to humour Kent and make sure that when the need arose its sympathies would be with them and not with any scheme to overthrow them.

Wordsworth, no doubt, had that consideration much in mind when he wrote:

> Vanguard of Liberty, ye men of Kent,
> Ye children of a soil that doth advance
> Her haughty brow against the coast of France . . .

In the sense that Kent is the only county of England that has the same boundaries today – give or take a parish! – as it had when it was first named one of King Alfred's shires, it can be said to be the oldest county in England. It is also the only one which has kept its name since the beginning of recorded history. The Romans found here the people they called the Cantii; the Jutes (Saxons) knew it as the territory of the Centingas, Cantguarlandt; the Domesday Book in 1086 called it Chent – near enough, wouldn't you say, to today's spelling, Kent?

Kent claims to be the first county of England, too, because the Jutes, under Hengist and Horsa, were the first of the Continental settlers after the Romans (who were never so much settlers as colonizers). The Jutes came from somewhere in what is now Northern Germany to this south-eastern corner of England some time before later arrivals, the Angles and the Saxons, settled in other parts of the country, and for that reason it is claimed for them that they were, in fact, the founders of the English nation.

After Hengist, there were, according to the eighteenth-century historian and topographer Edward Hasted, seventeen kings of Kent between 455 and 823, when Baldred was driven out by Egbert and England became one country. When Alfred the Great divided England into counties for administrative purposes, Kent was the only one of the ancient kingdoms that kept its old boundaries.

Kent is certainly one of the oldest inhabited parts of England, having once been connected to the Continental mainland by a land-bridge which hunters must have crossed. Those hunters almost certainly camped in what much later became Kent, centuries before the first settlers began living here permanently.

Julius Caesar reported that he found here in 54 BC a people called the Cantii, which he judged to be the most prosperous in Britain. That didn't seem to be saying very much, for he also wrote that the people dressed in skins and ate flesh, and he gave the impression that they were a pretty inferior lot, one way and another. Modern archaeologists, though, who might be credited with rather more long-sighted impartiality, point out that the Cantii in 54 BC Kent were well on the way to being pretty civilized by the standards of their day, whatever the Romans thought about them. They were certainly not wholly cut off from commerce with the Continental mainland and must have imported some of Roman Gaul's sophistication even before the Roman legions brought it with them on a more formal basis.

After the Romans left Britain, from AD 580 until he died, Ethelbert was Bretwalda or paramount king of all the Anglekin south of the Humber. But his own kingdom probably had almost identically the same shape as the geographical (not to be confused with the administrative) county has today.

That, then, is the historical and topographical framework within which the lore of Kent has been created.

Part of that lore is, in fact, the county badge, the rampant White Horse, which is certainly one of the most distinctive and dignified of all those adopted by the counties of England, and it may well be the oldest, too.

If Richard Verstegan was right when he wrote *A Restitution of Decayed Intelligence in Antiquities* in 1605, it was the Jutish chieftain brothers Hengist and Horsa who landed in Kent in AD 449 under the banner of a rampant white horse which was adapted as the badge of the kingdom and, later, of the county, after the Jutes had driven the Britons out.

That is certainly the most commonly accepted story today and, since no one can deny it, the one which has found its way into the common lore of Kent.

We know a little more certainly how the county motto '*Invicta*' was earned, although it would be too much to claim that legend, either, as anything much more substantial than just that. The word means simply 'Unconquered', and it supports Kent's claim to have survived the Norman Conquest without submitting to Norman William.

We have the word of a thirteenth-century Canterbury monk, Thomas Sprot, for that. Sprot wrote a chronicle in which he told how Archbishop Stigand and Abbot Egelsin led the Men of Kent to a great gathering near Swanscombe soon after William, Duke of Normandy, crowned himself King of England on Christmas Day 1066. The new King, of course, understood very well that he had to rule Kent if he was to rule England, and early in his reign he turned his attentions to the east and south of London.

Thus it was that, as he marched into Kent, he was met at Swanscombe by what apparently looked like a moving forest but which was, in fact, a (probably quite small) army of men all bearing green boughs. At a signal, the Men of Kent threw away the camouflaging greenery and revealed themselves, armed to the teeth. They offered William a choice. Either, they said, you allow Kent to keep its identity and its Saxon customs, or we offer you war – 'and that most deadly'.

William was no coward, but he was no fool, either. He countered: 'You surrender Dover Castle to me, and you can keep your ancient laws and customs, and enjoy a certain amount of independence – how's that?'

The Saxons knew that, while they might have taken a bit of the swagger out of the Normans that day, they could not now reverse what had already happened at Hastings and in London. William was King of England, however precariously, and so they struck the bargain, probably aware that it was as much as they could hope for and almost certainly more than they could expect to win in a fight. Besides, the Saxons were no fools themselves, and they may well already have had in mind the possibilities for claiming 'ancient rights' that they had not actually exercised with any legality hitherto.

So the Men of Kent put up their swords and went home, no doubt well enough pleased with themselves and boasting of how they had told that Norman bastard (for such, after all, he was!) just where he got off in good old no-nonsense Kentish Anglo-Saxon terms. On the strength of that day's work, whether or not it actually happened, Kent has ever since boasted that it was the one county in all England that was never conquered by the Normans – although, apart from being allowed to keep ancient customs that elsewhere died out and were supplanted by new ones, the boast was not perhaps quite as substantial as it might have been.

Twenty years later the Domesday Survey clerks were prying into Kent just as keenly as anywhere else, and the biggest bureaucratic land-grab in the country's history was pursued here no less than anywhere else.

One of the customs that survived in Kent, though, was the old Saxon practice of sharing an inheritance among all a man's children instead of, as was Norman custom, bequeathing the lot to the eldest. This had the effect of keeping the ancient Gavelkind practice in use in Kent – and only in Kent – right up to the present century, and incidentally added no end to the difficulties of historians trying to trace property ownerships.

Gavelkind was legal in Kent until 1925, and that was important to the county because it meant that land could not be forfeited at the will or whim of a local baron. It guaranteed, therefore, a vitally important stability of land-ownership that was lost in other parts of England. Gavelkind provided that, at the death of the owner, his property passed to all his surviving sons – and daughters – unless otherwise specifically willed.

So the feudal system which characterized the Norman hold on England never operated in Kent to the same extent as it did elsewhere.

Another of the ancient rights won from William promised that there should be no bondsmen or villeins (property-less peasants) in Kent, 'the bodies of all Kent people being free'. Which was all very well, and was useful in later bargaining with representatives of the Crown, but it did not stop the Domesday Surveyors noting the complement of villeins in each parish as they noted their way through Kent.

As well as its White Horse emblem, and its '*Invicta*' motto, Kent has another loreful characteristic that distinguishes it from all other counties. That is the tradition that the county is separated into two parts, East and West. It seems likely that that division is more than fifteen hundred years old and that it began after the Jutes left Thanet and settled into the serious business of taking over East Kent from the older Romano-Britons.

The original Jutish settlers sent back to their North European homelands for more colonizers to come and join them, and it was their arrival that brought a land-hunger that could only be satisfied by spreading westward. But by the time the decisive Battle of Aylesford was fought in 455, the new arrivals were coming from a different part of that homeland from the original immigrants and so were a different, although closely related, group of people.

Thus the division arose and the Jutes recognized the differences in the East Centingas and the West Centingas. The two have stayed separate, and there have been two Kent dioceses, Canterbury (East Kent) and Rochester (West Kent), since AD 605.

It is sometimes claimed that Shakespeare, in his play *King Henry VI*, first distinguished the Kentish Men from the Men of Kent in literature. But if, in fact, the Bard was consciously perpetuating a division that was well established within the county itself, then it has to be noted that he got it wrong.

In Act III of Part II, he had the Duke of York speak of 'a headstrong Kentishman, John Cade of Ashford'. In fact, of course, anyone from Ashford (East Kent) would have been a Man of Kent. Elsewhere throughout the play various characters refer to 'Kentish rebels', and in Scene viii of Act IV Lord Say addresses 'You Men of Kent . . .'.

So it seems that the Bard was not altogether clear whether he meant the Men of (East) Kent or the (West) Kentish Men, and may well have been merely the victim of the dilemma into which Kent puts all who try to speak or write of all her people at once. There is no convenient way of lumping the county's natives together without using the 'ish' or the 'of' which, in fact, separates them.

The Honourable Society of the Natives of Kent was formed in London in 1657 with the object of helping with the education of Men of Kent and Kentish Men in London, and 'keeping in remembrance the great traditions of the county.'

The Association of Men of Kent and Kentish Men, which still exists today, was formed in December 1897 at a meeting at Holborn Viaduct Hotel, London. Today the Association meets in Kent and has its headquarters in the county town of Maidstone. Its badge, an upraised arm holding a sword rising from a circlet of green boughs, itself commemorates the '*Invicta*' legend and perpetuates the report that this was the crest of the Kentish bowmen at Agincourt.

It was at Ebbsfleet in Kent that Augustine and his monks landed in 597 and, with the baptism of King Ethelbert that same summer, put Kent in the forefront of the new Christian era in Britain and set the scene for Canterbury to become the religious centre of southern England and, later, of the whole nation.

There was a brief period when it seemed unlikely that that

would ever happen. After Ethelbert's death, his son Eadbald abandoned his parents' faith and returned to heathen practices. Archbishop Laurentius, who succeeded Augustine, felt that all the good work of his predecessor had been wasted, and would have abandoned his mission and gone home to Rome had not (thus the lore, at any rate) the Apostle Peter come to him one night and scourged him for even thinking of deserting God's flock and told him to go to the King and preach the true faith to him.

Laurentius must have put his affairs in order before he obeyed that particular command, fully expecting that he was setting out to preach his last sermon on earth. But, in fact, the King heard him and was persuaded to embrace Christianity as his father had done, and Kent – not to mention the King and, of course, Archbishop Laurentius! – was saved.

Nevertheless, despite Kent's undoubted precedence as the seat of the country's Primate, it was not always the peak of ambition for churchmen to become Archbishop of Canterbury. Kent was, from Roman times, reckoned to be a favoured and cultured corner of the kingdom, and there was a saying, 'Neither in Kent nor in Christendom,' which meant that, if something was not known or to be found in Kent, it was unlikely to be found anywhere else.

Yet one Bishop of Winchester is remembered for his refusal to accept the Archbishopric of Canterbury with the words: 'Canterbury is the higher rack, but Winchester the better manger.' By which it is supposed that he meant that, although Canterbury had the higher status, Winchester offered the better living.

A peculiarly Kentish custom is the characteristic applause of acclamation known as Kentish Fire. This is a peculiar style of rhythmic hand-clapping, two slow, three quick, repeated. The origins are obscure but may have been Continental, brought to Kent by the Huguenot refugees in the seventeenth century. Certainly, something very similar is to be heard on the Continent today.

The first recorded use of the term in Kent was in October 1828 when a reported fifty thousand men gathered on Penenden Heath, just outside Maidstone, led by the High Sheriff of Kent, to petition Parliament against the Catholic Emancipation Bill. In 1834 Lord Winchilsea, in proposing a toast to the Earl of Roden, said: 'Let it be given with the Kentish Fire' – and that seems to be the first record of Kentish Fire accompanying a toast.

Today Kentish Fire is most often heard at traditional county ceremonies when dignitaries like the Lord Lieutenant, the High Sheriff or mayors of the county's boroughs are welcomed by the assembly and/or as they leave at the end of the ceremony.

There are other traditions that Kent used to claim for her own but which are now almost completely forgotten. There used to be a game called Stroke-Bias played mainly in East Kent which seems to have been a local variation of goal-running. Exactly what were the rules or even the objects of the game seem to have been forgotten, but evidently it was played by members of two or more villages competing, and it depended to a very large extent upon the speed, agility and endurance of the players. It seems likely that it was a fairly punishing game physically and that a certain amount of what is nowadays known as body contact was normal.

Bat and trap is another game that Kent claims as its own. This is still played today, and there is a pubs league. The game dates from at least the fourteenth century and may be much older than that. It is played with a racquet-shaped bat eighteen inches long and a hard rubber ball. The ball is placed on one end of a see-saw board in a box-like trap, and the other end of the see-saw is struck with the edge of the bat, sending the ball into the air, to be hit with the flat of the bat. The object is to hit it between two poles, thirteen feet six inches apart, at the far end of a twenty-one-yards-long pitch.

If the ball is caught by one of the fielders, the batsman is out and there is no score. If the ball does not go through the poles, it is picked up by each of the fielding side in turn and bowled back at the trap in an attempt to hit it. While this is going on, the batsman must not defend the trap, and if it is hit, then the batsman is out.

If the ball is successfully hit between the poles, one point is scored for the batting side, but if the batsman misses the ball after he has put it into play by striking the ball-less end of the see-saw board, he is out.

It is, in fact, a game perfectly suited to fairly small pieces of ground at the back of a country pub, where it demands just enough of players and spectators to give them a thirst without demanding enough to make temperance among the players at all necessary.

Perhaps Kent once had other games and pastimes, customs

and practices that were peculiar to itself. If so, they would seem to have passed out of use and not to have been remembered in lore. Which is unusual. So much of what was once, even if only for a short period, the everyday commonplace of the lives of ordinary people – whether it was in their work or their play or their convictions or their gossip – subsides as soon as it is no longer current into lore where it lives on to give a depth of consciousness to each new generation.

There is no such thing as lore enforcement, but there are penalties for those who do not keep the lore and the fines are heavy – nothing less, indeed, than the riches of a priceless heritage which, once lost, can never be recovered.

2

Lore and Language

Dialect is important to lore because, of course, most lore started as speech and was passed down from generation to generation by word of mouth before ever it was committed to paper. In a sense, dialect is as much a part of the body of lore as the tales in which it is told. So it is necessary to have at least an inkling of the dialect of Kent in order to get the fullest flavour of county lore.

The authentic old Kentish dialect is not easy to find any more. You may yet hear it in a few of the more remotely rural parts of East Kent and the Weald, but you need a quick ear to discern it.

Kent has always been a haven for refugees, both from persecutions of one sort or another in other lands and also from the rigours and distractions of less favoured parts of England, too. As one of the Home Counties it has, since even before the railways began to popularize travel to an extent undreamed-of before them, been a refuge for Londoners seeking solace from the city's stresses. Today, most of North and West Kent and quite a lot of the county further east as well is comfortably within London's commuter belt, so that it sometimes seems difficult to find a Kent-born native at all, far less one whose speech has been unchanged by the combined efforts of education, social intercourse and the broadcasting media, radio or television.

Each of those has contributed, not only in Kent, of course, to smoothing out all sorts of local distinguishing sights and sounds, but especially sounds. A few uniquely Kentish expressions linger a little more tenaciously than most, but they grow fewer with each passing generation. The influence of London on the county's vocal chords is more pronounced now than it ever was, even before commuting became a way of life for many thousands of Kent's residents.

In many parts of Kent it is the accents of London that dominate everyday speech patterns. The London English of Lambeth and Southwark came into the Weald with the hundreds of thousands of the city's poorest people who made the pilgrimage every year to the hop gardens and fruit orchards throughout the nineteenth and well into the twentieth century. Later, those same people came by trains, on cheap day excursions, as poverty on the old scale succumbed more and more to relative affluence. Later still, in retirement, they came back to try to recapture those holiday visits and settled in some of the seaside towns, so that the Isle of Thanet particularly has been labelled, a little undeservedly, a geriatric ghetto.

Then, like other waves of settlers before them – Jutes and Danes, Flemings and Huguenots – they sent back to their homelands word of the delights of their new home and made it an El Dorado, a promised land, for others who followed them.

These people will tell you, in accents that belie their words, though not the conviction with which they are spoken, that they are Kentish, thus adding to the bewilderment of the outsider in search of the true Kentish dialect.

Perhaps the attitudes of the natives are more discernible today than the sounds they make. The true Kentish Man – and it is even more true of the Man of Kent – finds it difficult to adjust to the idea that there is anything much worth bothering about to the north and west of London. He does not actually draw a circle on his maps beyond which he writes merely, 'Here Be Dragons.' But he is, even today, very apt to dismiss anywhere beyond, say, East Sussex, Surrey, London and Essex with a vague acknowledgement that there are settlements out there but that since that is not his fault he cannot be expected to spare more than a very little passing sympathy for the people who live in them.

Indeed, he will speak with much more conviction and even warmth about France than he will about, say, Bedfordshire or Lincoln. It has nothing to do with his knowledge or ignorance of English geography. Even the most widely travelled Kent people often have very little 'feel' for the rest of England. They know it is there, but they have never felt the least need to consider it because it seems to have nothing very much to do with them.

This very widespread attitude is in large part a fairly natural consequence of living in a corner of the country, many parts of which are physically nearer to France than they are even to London. It is only very recently indeed that more than a few of the trade links of Kent have been with anywhere other than France and London. The London-Dover road was one of the glamour routes of the old coaching days. Prestige expresses like the

Golden Arrow travelled the same corridor of communication in the true (as distinct from the advertised) age of the train.

Now that roads are back in favour, the county's only two motorways incompletely but unarguably stress the London-France link, and if the Channel tunnel is ever built, that will underline it still more.

No wonder, then, that modern Kent still perpetuates, in attitude of mind even if not in spoken words any longer, the conviction that anyone from anywhere beyond Sussex and London is 'from the Sheers' (the Shires) – an old expression that is pretty well lost now, although the vague wave of the hand and the blank expression that accompanied it survive to accompany whatever more modern expression is used instead.

Perhaps the last communal custodians of the Kentish dialect are the county's gipsies, many of whom have travelled all over the county but may have ventured outside it only as far as East Sussex or the South London boroughs in the whole of their lives. Many of them still lead a life that is predominantly agricultural or horticultural, travelling from farm to farm throughout the summer and in the winter seeking forestry or land-clearing work. Many of them even today cannot read or write, and their nomadic existence keeps them insulated from the changes that have taken place among more settled communities.

Luckily, however, Kent does not have to rely on the gipsies, whose lifestyle is changing, although more slowly than that of most of us, to keep the county dialect intact. Even if the authentic old dialect vanished completely, its words would not be completely lost, thanks to a long dialect poem called *Dick and Sal at Canterbury Fair*, which was written early in the nineteenth century and published some time before 1821. It is a good deal more valuable for the dialect it rather self-consciously enshrines in its hundred four-line verses than for its poetic qualities, but especially if you have a copy that is annotated with explanations of some of the more obscure words and phrases, it gives a very good idea of one particular aspect of life in rural Kent in former times, told in the words still current at the time.

In the poem, Dick is a bailiff's boy, who recounts to milkmaid Mary a visit he made to Canterbury Fair with a young woman called Sal. We are not told explicitly what is the relationship between the two. It might have been that they were brother and sister, although at the fair she is referred to as Dick's wife without contradiction. However, it is not a matter that affects the narrative very much.

The week-long fair was evidently a hiring fair, at which farm workers offered their services to prospective employers by carrying a 'shining stick', a thin wand with the bark peeled off, signifying that they were looking for work. Employers needing workers would approach likely looking stick-carriers, many of whom would be known to them from previous years, and offer them terms and conditions that would be haggled over and either accepted or refused.

Anyway, Dick and Sal set off. 'De Folkston gals looked houghed black' (Folkston gals – rain clouds; houghed – a fairly mild expletive, probably roughly equivalent to 'confoundedly'), but Sal notices '. . . the lark is mountain high, De clouds to underline,' so she concludes that the clouds would clear and it would be fine later on. Sure enough, as they went on,

> 'De rain an wind we left behind,
> De clouds was scar'd away,
> Bright Pebus he shut-fisted shin'd,
> And 'twas a lightful day.'

Their way took them through Perry 'ood (wood), Stone Stile and then by the turnpike road through Shanford Street, and over Chartham Down into Canterbury by way of Wincheap. Today we could assume that their starting-point was the village of Selling (between Faversham and Chilham) and that their way took them through Perry Wood (which is still so called) and the hamlet of Stone Stile (also still there) and onto the road through what is now Shalmsford Street and Chartham, a walk of about ten miles, perhaps a bit less if you know the short cuts.

Arrived in the great city, the adventurous couple spent the day seeing the sights, and, as Dick said,

> 'I lay dat dare was more
> Houses an churches den we'd sin
> In all 'ur lives afore.'

They saw all sorts of other things, too, including a book shop which enticed Sal inside.

> 'Sal, ye see, had bin ta school
> She went to old aunt Kite;

> An so she was'en quite a fool,
> But cud read purty tight.'

They had a job making the woman in the shop understand what they wanted, but at last they bought their book, which became a family favourite when they took it home with them.

After a dinner of ale and steaks they went in search of the fair. A man they knew became too familiar with Sal for Dick's liking, and Dick knocked him down, whereupon the other man picked himself up and 'knockt me throught de winder'. After that things got out of hand a bit.

> 'I claw'd hold av his mane,
> An mint ta fetch his head a cuff,
> But brok anudder pane.

> 'Den I was up, den I gun swear,
> De chaps dey did just laught,
> An Sal she stompt, an tore har hair,
> An beller'd like a calf.'

The owner of the shop whose windows had suffered demanded recompense, and, after arguing that the other fellow had started the fight and should pay for the damage, Dick finally 'dobb'd him down the stuff,

> A plaguey sight to pay;
> An Sal an I was glad enuff
> At last ta git away.'

There were all sorts of fun and games at the fair.

> 'My nable! there was lots of fun,
> An such hubbub an hollar;
> De donkeys dey for cheeses run,
> An I grinn'd through a collar.
> Den Sal she run for half-a-crown,
> An I jumpt in a sack,
> An shoud'd a won, but I fell down,
> An gran nigh brok my back.'

At last Sal said she'd seen enough. It was almost 'sebb'm'

(seven) by then, and after Dick had bought Sal a ribbon by which to remember the day, they left Canterbury and walked back home again.

Very few of the dialect expressions and phrases used in the poem remain in use today. But there are some expressions which Kent claims as her own which you will hear still now and again. For instance, parents still chide their children for 'keeping all on acting about', and countrymen crossing a field from one corner to another, diagonally, talk of going 'caterways'. Kentish ants are still 'ammuts'; a ditch a 'dick', and you may still hear a great number of anything called 'a rare daffy'.

It is an odd thing about dialect: the people who use it naturally never think of it as anything extraordinary or distinguishing. They take it for granted and suppose that it is the way people everywhere speak. I remember the first time I picked up a book called *A Dictionary of the Kentish Dialect and Provincialisms in use in the County of Kent*, by W. D. Parish (Chancellor of Chichester Cathedral and Vicar of Selmerston) and W. F. Shaw (Vicar of Eastry, Kent), and published for the English Dialect Society in 1887. I was genuinely astonished to find that words I had used unself-consciously all my life had been marking me as a Kentish-man despite all the best efforts of education to eradicate any such identity. (My schooling ended just before it began to be fashionable to be proud of regional accents.)

At home, for instance, Monday was always 'banyan day' – a busy day for Mother and therefore a day when dinner was always a quick and easily prepared meal, often concocted from left-over odds and ends from the weekend meals. It usually included 'fryers-up' (bubble and squeak), though whether 'fryers-up' was a Kentish rather than a family expression I'm still not sure, having only once ever come across it outside my own home.

My grandfather, I remember well, always answered enquiries about his health by replying that he was 'amongst the middlin's, ya know,' by which he meant that he couldn't complain.

I took it for granted that fractious children 'kicked up a dido' when they created a noisy disturbance; and we never hoped something would happen: we were always 'in hopes' that it would.

Years ago, the county newspaper of Kent, the old broadsheet *Kent Messenger*, used to have a Children's Corner which was always called 'Keg-Megs'. The initials were appropriate, of course, but it took my *Dictionary of Kentish Dialect* to tell me that the expression itself was a Kentish dialect one meaning gossips or news-mongers.

It never used to rain hard in Kent; always 'heavens hard'. Nothing ever happened later; always 'not yet awhile'. Anything that was a bit of a performance – a lot of fuss over nothing very much – was always dismissed as 'a right old menagerie, an no mistake', and children who teased other children or animals were admonished: 'Do stop keep all on terrifying the life out of him!'

The word 'loo' has become a fashionable commonplace substitute for lavatory, yet in fact it is an update of an old Anglo-Saxon word that may have come to these islands with the Jutes of Hengist and Horsa, more than fifteen hundred years ago, when it was an everyday word meaning simply shelter.

Kentish children never crunch sweets; they always scrunch them. Just as they always scrumple up the sweet paper, rather than crumpling it. Anyone who eats his food fast may still be told not to 'scoff it down' like that. Similarly, noisy drinkers may yet be called 'old sozzle-pots', although the dialect word 'sozzle' was also used to describe the process of cooling tea by tipping it back and forth from cup to saucer, saucer to cup – a practice which has, itself, pretty well died out now, I think.

Of anything at all doubtful, Kentish people still 'lay' it will or will not happen: 'I lay that'll rain 'fore long.' (To which the reply will very likely be, because we are also a contrary people: 'That won't rain yet awhile, I lay!')

In a county that has been predominantly agricultural for so long, it would be odd if there were not some uniquely Kentish expressions for farming practices, and indeed there are. Any dry timber, that is timber that is not actually green, is always spoken of as 'sere', and the same word signifies in dialect any fabric that is rotten or worn. Fruit, in this major fruit-growing county, always hangs from its branch by the strig (not the stalk) and is harvested and paid for by the sieve or half-sieve, a sieve being a bushel of fifty-six pounds. Peas and beans grow in shucks rather than husks or shells, and the old-fashioned sheaves of corn were always shocked up, not stacked.

Kent is also the major hop-growing county of England, and the hop gardens (which, incidentally, are never hop yards or hop grounds or even just hop fields, as they are elsewhere) have been responsible for a lot of expressions in Kent that are not heard elsewhere. Many of them are dying out now because they were used by the old hop-pickers who have been ousted by the machines. Nevertheless, hops are always grown in hills (usually four plants to a hill), which are themselves calculated in sets, with twenty-four hills to the set.

An old hop-picking custom was that of greeting visitors to the garden by brushing their shoes with a branch of hops and demanding shoe-money for the service. The money was then donated towards the cost of the traditional end-of-hopping 'bean-feast'.

Today, when recalling in cold blood these expressions which were common enough still forty years ago gives them a strange sound to my ears, I know that, when I am momentarily lost for words in an emotional crisis, I revert to using them. No doubt the same is true of a lot of natives of the county, who have dropped these colloquialisms from their everyday speech for all sorts of reasons of which they are totally unconscious most of the time.

But there are many people for whom they are conversational currency still, if you can but find them. For my part, at least, long may it be so.

3

Lore Abiding

An enormous amount of local lore clusters around real people and real events in which those people were involved during their lifetimes. Often, records of those events are fragmentary or tantalizingly cryptic, and the full stories have had to be pieced together wherever possible. Sometimes it has not been possible, and then we must fall back upon lore – the handed-down stories which can be accepted as true in the absence of any evidence to the contrary.

The Biddenden Maids, Eliza and Mary Chulkhurst, are a good example. They were real people, although we know very little about their lives. They were born, probably in about 1100 (despite the anachronistic costume in which they are represented on the famous Biddenden village sign), in the parish of Biddenden in the Weald of Kent. They were Siamese twins, possibly England's first and certainly the first we know about, and they lived together in the most complete sense possible, joined at shoulder and hip, for thirty-four years. Then, one of them was taken ill and died. The survivor refused to allow her sister to be removed from her side by surgery and, within a few hours, she too died, declaring that they had come into the world together and now they must leave it the same way.

They were the daughters of a prosperous local farmer, and when they died they bequeathed land in the parish to provide a dole of money and food for the local poor – a dole that is perpetuated still in the local Bread and Cheese Lands (now built upon) and the annual dole of purpose-baked and very durable (not to say inedible!) biscuits stamped with a representation of the twins themselves.

The Peasants' Revolt of 1381 is fully accepted as history, but what we know of how it began depends very heavily upon lore. It is generally said that the rebellion was led by a man called Wat Tyler of Dartford. In fact, there is a good deal of historical doubt about that. Some say that the Wat Tyler who played a leading role in the events of that summer was not the original instigator and that, in any case, he came from Essex – although that does not mean he was not working in Dartford at the time.

It is legend rather than history, again, that claims the revolt was sparked off when Tyler killed a tax-man who manhandled his daughter while making up his mind whether or not she was old enough to be liable for poll-tax payment.

What happened after that is rather more certain. Kentish Men downed tools by the thousand and went on the rampage. They overran Rochester and then gathered on one of Kent's traditional stamping grounds, Penenden Heath near Maidstone, where on 7 June they elected Wat Tyler their leader. Their ranks swelled by the Maidstone men, the rebels next marched on Canterbury, took the city and forced Sheriff William Septvans to take their own rebel oath.

Then they burned records in the Archbishop's palace, and Tyler himself declared from the cathedral pulpit that Archbishop Simon of Sudbury, who as Chancellor had introduced the hated poll tax, would be executed when found.

Thoroughly roused by now, the peasants freed the rebel priest John Ball from the Archbishop's prison at Maidstone on their way to a great gathering, a hundred thousand strong, from all the Home Counties, on Blackheath.

There, it seems, King Richard's mother, Joan the first Fair Maid of Kent and widow of the Black Prince, came upon the mob as she returned to London from a pilgrimage to Canterbury, but the rebels had no grudge against her, or, indeed, her royal son, but only against his ministers and advisers. Joan was allowed to pass freely, although she was subjected to a few affectionate if disrespectful kisses as she did so.

Later, after the rebels became the only attackers ever to take the Tower of London, where they beheaded Archbishop Simon and Sir John Hales, Treasurer of England, they again allowed Joan to escape unharmed.

The rebellion ended when the Mayor of London, William Walworth (another Dartford man, by the way), stabbed the rebel leader, who fell mortally wounded in front of the whole crowd and at the feet of his King. When the rebels, almost to a man, accepted the King's immediate invitation to acknowledge him as their new leader, Tyler's head was struck off and spiked.

Quite a lot of what we know of Joan, that first Fair Maid of Kent, is lore rather than history, too. She was probably born in about 1328, the daughter of Edmund, Earl of Kent, half-brother to Edward II. Edmund was executed by order of Queen Isabella and Lord Mortimer in 1330, and it was after that, probably in 1339, that Joan secretly married Thomas Holland. The marriage remained secret for eight years. Holland fought with the Black Prince at Crécy, and the two were friends, but the Prince knew nothing of the secret marriage when in 1341 Edward III arranged for Joan to be married to Montague, Earl of Salisbury.

Holland had then to disclose his own marriage and sued for pardon. It was, of course, a major scandal, and a papal court of inquiry was set up to inquire into whether or not the Hollands were legally married. In 1349 a Papal Bull declared that Holland was, in truth, the lawful husband of Joan, and the King accepted that. Holland was one of the initial Knights of the Garter, and he became Earl of Kent in 1353. He died in Normandy in 1360 and was buried in Lincolnshire. The next year, Edward the Black Prince married Joan. The wedding, according to contemporary chroniclers, was performed by four bishops, one abbot and 'a leash of deans'. It was, for all we know to the contrary, a happy match, but not a long one. The Prince died in 1376, and it was his son, and Joan's, Richard of Bordeaux, who succeeded to the throne as Richard II. Joan died in 1385.

If you visit the parish church of St Mary of Charity at Faversham, you may see what is said to be the final resting place of King Stephen (1135–54) and his queen Matilda. But nobody knows if the royal remains really do RIP in the church. We do know that Stephen founded the great Cluniac abbey at Faversham which flourished until the Dissolution in the 1530s. We know, too, that he intended that he and his queen should be buried there, and that it was his hope that their son Eustace would succeed him and in due course be buried at Faversham also.

But Stephen's reign was a troubled one, and things did not work out the way he hoped. For a start, his son died before either he or Matilda did. He was buried in the abbey, and so, in their turn, were Stephen and Matilda.

That much is fairly certain. But at the time of the Dissolution, tradition asserts, local people rifled the abbey tombs for the lead and other saleable materials and then tipped the bones inside them into the nearby creek. They treated the remains of the royal family with no more respect than those of everybody else, but legend claims that others came along afterwards and retrieved the bones of Stephen and his queen and reinterred them in the church.

Another legend concerning a royal corpse grew up around the tomb of Henry IV in Canterbury Cathedral. It claimed that, after the King's death in 1413, his body was being carried by sea from London to Faversham in order to go on from there to Canterbury in accordance with the royal wish, a storm arose and, to lighten ship, the body was thrown overboard and never reached the cathedral tomb. This tradition persisted for four hundred years until the tomb (incidentally, the only tomb of an English king in the cathedral) was finally opened in 1832 in order to find out if the story were true or not. Inside the tomb, two lead coffins were found. In one were two twigs tied together into the form of a cross. An oval peephole was cut in the second coffin, and when the investigators looked through it, the King's face, instantly recognizable from the likeness of the effigy on the tomb itself, was glimpsed, with a thick beard of a deep russet colour. As soon as the air got to it, the face disintegrated and the evidence was gone, but by then so was the legend, and once again history had triumphed over lore.

The fifteenth-century leader of the second great Kentish Revolt, Jack Cade, may have been a rascally trouble-maker, was almost certainly not a native of Kent and was quite likely a hired rabble-rouser who deserved very little of the acclaim he gained during those few midsummer days in 1450.

Shakespeare, in his play *Henry VI* (Part II), had the Duke of York speak of Cade as a Kentishman from Ashford – which in itself only goes to show what can happen when a native of Warwickshire writes speeches for a Duke of York about a man from East Kent where, as every Kentishman knows, they are all Men of Kent.

What is certain is that, when the people of Kent rebelled against the corrupt and tyrannical government of Henry VI at Whitsun 1450, Cade emerged as spokesman and leader. He sent a petition to the King in which he called himself 'The Captain of the great Assembly in Kent'. Taking the name of John Mortimer and claiming kinship with the family of that name, the self-styled Captain of Kent assembled twenty thousand followers on Blackheath ready to march on London to seek royal redress for their grievances.

The rebels easily routed a small force of king's men near Sevenoaks and then, reinforced with malcontents from other south-eastern counties, marched on to find the City gates opened to them by the Londoners. The Lord Lieutenant of Kent, Lord Saye and Sele of Knole, and his son-in-law William Crowmer, Sheriff of Kent, were both seized by the rebels and beheaded, and after that Cade's control over the mob began to slip. There was looting and an all-night battle for London Bridge which the Londoners won, after which a truce was called and a pardon proclaimed for all rebels who would go home.

Many did. Cade withdrew via Southwark to Rochester, where he sacrificed his pardon by attacking the castle, and then, an outlaw now, he rode for Lewes in Sussex. Quite how he met his end is in some doubt, although in Kent we assert that he was killed by the new Sheriff of Kent, Alexander Iden, on the Kentish side of the Sussex border.

We have the word of the man himself that William Caxton, introducer of printing to England, was born in the Weald of Kent. Unfortunately, he left us no more precise information about where in the Weald it was, but Tenterden has long claimed the distinction of being his birthplace during the first half of the 1420s.

Suggestions that he meant the village of Weald, near Sevenoaks, are generally dismissed in East Kent as a fairly clumsy attempt by the Kentish Men to claim Caxton as one of them. There are a number of gaps in our knowledge of Caxton's early life, although it seems he lived abroad for some twenty-five years and was ambassador for Edward IV in Bruges for part of that time.

When he came home in 1476, he set up his own press near Westminster Abbey and became the first English commercial publisher. He didn't exactly flood the market with books even then. Printing was still a slow business, even though it was faster than copying by hand, and books were expensive. But it did bring an urgent need for order into the fairly chaotic written English of Caxton's day. Fifteenth-century written English was a rude sort of tool. Words meant pretty much what their authors decided they should mean, and Latin and French words and phrases abounded as the only way of expressing some ideas at all. Spelling was totally undisciplined. If only in the commercial interests of the mass production of books, even on the fifteenth-century scale, that had to change.

So Caxton, simply by making up his own rules based on the 'broad and rude' (his own words) dialect of the Weald of Kent and spreading his version of the language in his printed books, imposed that dialect on the rest of England, at least to some extent. There have, of course, been other influences at work, but since all things spring from that which has gone before, we may claim, here in Kent, that it was our dialect that shaped the King's English, thanks to Master Caxton, the printer.

One of the most appealing of all Kent legends – for, really, it is no more than that – is that which surrounds the reputed tomb of Richard Plantagenet in the ruins of the church at Eastwell, between Ashford and Faversham.

The register of the parish tells barely that Richard Plantagenet was buried there on 22 December. The rest of the story is the handed-down account, said to have been given to the first owner of Eastwell House by one of his stonemasons who claimed to be the illegitimate son of Richard III.

According to the story, when the house was being built by Sir Thomas Moyle, one of the stonemasons was seen to take every opportunity to steal away for a few moments to read a book which he carried with him always. Intrigued, Sir Thomas made it his business to find out more about this book, and when he discovered that it was written in Latin, his curiosity could not be contained any longer. Only the well-educated could read Latin, and the well-educated did not usually include elderly stonemasons. He asked the man outright how he came to be able to read such books.

The explanation that the old man gave might well have been little more than a belated opportunity snatched to make a mark on the world. But it might equally have been the true story of a man who had kept quiet for long enough and who was now old enough not to care any more what the consequences of revealing his secret might be.

He said he had been brought up by a woman he believed was his mother until, at the age of seven, he was boarded with a Latin schoolmaster in the country somewhere. While he was there, he had no knowledge of any kin, and he never had any visitors except for a gentleman who came once a quarter to pay his bills for him. When he was sixteen, that gentleman took him away to a great house where someone who wore a Garter Star spoke kindly to him and gave him ten gold pieces before he was taken back to school.

Some time later, the same gentleman took him to Leicester, where he was taken to King Richard's tent on Bosworth Field. The King embraced him and told him he was his true father.

'Watch the battle from a safe place tomorrow,' the King instructed him. 'If I win, come to me afterwards and I will claim you as my son. If I lose, you must shift for yourself as best you can, but be sure not to let anyone know who your father was, for no mercy will be shown to any son of mine!'

The King then gave the young man a purse of gold, and he was conducted to a safe place from which to watch the battle. In the event, the King lost and was killed, and the boy hurried back to London where he sold his house and the fine clothes his royal father's money had bought, and apprenticed himself to a bricklayer. But although he embraced anonymity as a life-preserver, he never lost the love of books his upbringing had given him. By the time Sir Thomas found him out at Eastwell, he was an old man, and Sir Thomas offered him comfort for the rest of his days, supervising the work in the kitchen of the new house.

But the old man said he was used to living alone and wanted no change. He begged to be allowed just to live out his life in the little one-room cottage he had built for himself in a nearby field, and that permission was given. It was in that cottage (long since gone, of course) that he died. The field in which the cottage stood became part of the newly enclosed Eastwell Park.

Richard Plantagenet, if his story was true, was probably about eighty when he died a few years after he told his story to Sir Thomas.

Then there was the strange case of Elizabeth Barton of Aldington. Was she, indeed, the Holy Maid of Kent – or a poor creature who suffered from delusions and who was taken advantage of for political reasons? We shall never really know. We do know that she emerged from anonymity into history as the servant of Thomas Cobb, bailiff to the Archbishop of Canterbury. In 1525 she suffered a severe illness during which she lapsed into fever often and began to make predictions. Even after she recovered from the illness, the ability to predict events remained with her, it seems.

The local rector took an interest in the girl and declared that he had absolute faith in her predictions, as a result of which the reputation of Elizabeth Barton began to spread and she became something of a celebrity. The rector, a man named Richard

Master, decided that he should consult the Archbishop about her, and the Archbishop appointed a commission to investigate the case to see if the girl was, indeed, specially blessed or only commonly cursed.

Perhaps all this untoward attention went to Elizabeth's head. Perhaps – for there really are more things in heaven and earth . . . – she told the simple truth. Whichever, she claimed that she was commanded directly by the Virgin Mary to enter a convent, and Archbishop Warham, no doubt resorting to the better-safe-than-sorry principle, arranged for her entry into the convent of St Sepulchre near Canterbury.

There her reputation for holiness continued to grow, and she began to prophesy against King Henry VIII's proposal to divorce his queen and marry Anne Boleyn of Hever. This is where many people since have decided the poor girl was being used to voice views held by politicians concerned for the effects of the King's actions. However it really was, Elizabeth found herself caught up in a highly dangerous web from which she seemed powerless to escape, or else unaware of the almost inevitable end that awaited her.

Towards the end of 1533 several of the Archbishop's commissioners of inquiry were arrested. So was Elizabeth. There was a show trial, at which the prisoners were accused of plotting treason together, found guilty and condemned. On the scaffold, Elizabeth made a 'confession' before she was hanged and decapitated so that her head could be displayed on London Bridge.

History records the ignominious death of a traitor, however deserving of that taint she may have been; Kentish lore remembers the Holy Maid of Kent and never asks if the title was deserved or not.

History can tell us a great deal about Christopher Marlowe, the Canterbury-born playwright who, some would have us believe, was the more likely author of some of the works since credited to William Shakespeare. But it is lore and very little more that tells us that Kit Marlowe lived another, secret life which led to his being killed at the tragically early age of only twenty-eight.

Marlowe was, we know, born in the same year as Shakespeare, 1564, son of a Canterbury shoemaker and City alderman. He went to King's School, Canterbury, and then to Cambridge, where he took a BA degree in 1584 and his MA in 1587. He quickly distinguished himself as a Latin scholar and poet of genius, as well as a lively, likeable character, full of the spirit of adventure that strutted through the Renaissance period both here and on the Continent.

It is easy enough to believe that he was a willing recruit to the highly organized and probably well-paid secret service master-minded by Sir Francis Walsingham. At any rate, while he was still at Cambridge, it seems he quite frequently crossed to the Low Countries on unexplained missions that could have been connected with such activities.

He had a madcap lust for life that would never be wholly burned up by the business of setting words down on paper, nor in acting them out on a stage, although he did both brilliantly. He lived in roistering times, and young Kit Marlowe roistered with the best of his contemporaries.

His untimely death was the result (it is usually assumed) of a drunken brawl in a Deptford bawdy house, where, apparently, he came to blows with three men and was killed when his own drawn dagger was turned against him and he was stabbed through the eye.

There was some evidence and a lot of gossip that, in fact, he was the victim of a political assassination, possibly staged to seem to be a spontaneous brawl. The other three men involved were arrested, questioned and pardoned. There was no public trial, and at least one of the three was known to have been involved in diplomatic intrigue.

Naturally, when the law is vague in detail, the lore is quick to fill the gaps, and today Kit Marlowe, secret agent, is probably rather better remembered than Christopher Marlowe, man of letters.

Incidentally, one of several mysteries surrounding the life and death of Marlowe is the one of what he looked like. The portrait that was found among rubbish at Cambridge could be of him, as was claimed, but there is no way of being certain of it. Perhaps if he had lived longer we might have known more about him from clues scattered through his work. As it is, Marlowe the mystery man belongs almost as much to the Lore of Kent as he does to the literary history of England.

One of those appealing little fragments of lore that sometimes cling to even the historically well-documented people is the story that is told of a member of the Wyatt family, Sir Henry Wyatt, first owner in the family of Allington Castle, just down river from Maidstone, and now, in fact, part of the borough.

The Wyatts had a pretty tempestuous history, one way or another. It was the two Sir Thomases, father and son, both born at Allington who are probably best remembered.

The elder, born in 1503, was a scholar, courtier and poet, Sheriff of Kent, twice King Henry VIII's Minister at the Spanish Court, and Ambassador-Extraordinary to the Court of Charles V in France and Belgium. Yet, after all that, he probably left his most indelible mark on history by dying in 1542 as a result – it was claimed – of hurrying too fast to answer a royal summons.

His only son, the younger Sir Thomas, was a problem child from the start. A good deal of what we know of him is lore, leaked out from between chinks in the carefully censored history of his influential family. It has been suggested that he was married off at the age of fifteen or sixteen in the hope that marriage might settle him down a bit. It didn't. Six years after the wedding he made over some family estates in Dorset to his natural son by a west country girl, and a year later, in 1543, he was imprisoned for breaking windows in London one night with stones shot from a crossbow.

When he was released, he found an outlet for his restlessness by leading a private army to France, where he joined forces with Charles V in the successful siege of Landracy, and distinguished himself well enough to earn the job of Governor of Boulogne.

When he returned home, he was soon in trouble with the Privy Council, which accused him of having taken up arms in support of Lady Jane Grey. He was acquitted, but in 1554 he led a Kentish rising against the proposed marriage of Queen Mary to Philip, future king of Spain. The banner of that rebellion was raised on 25 January on Penenden Heath, ancient rallying place for Kentish rebels of all kinds, and the following day he stormed and took Rochester Castle. He went on to take Cooling Castle before he marched on London, where, barred from entering the city at London Bridge, he went on to cross the Thames at Kingston instead.

Unhappily for him, his supporters were less dedicated than he was, and by the time he marched into the City of London, he had only a very small band of men behind him. The little band of insurrectionists was surrounded at Temple Bar, and Wyatt was arrested. He was beheaded on Tower Hill on 11 April, aged thirty-four, and his head was set up on a pole in Hyde Park but was stolen by sympathizers.

Practically all the rebellion achieved was the death by hanging of some 150 of the insurgents, some in London, others in Kent, and the withdrawal of Maidstone's charter for five years. Queen Mary did, after all, marry Philip of Spain.

But to return to the earlier Sir Henry Wyatt and the story that, perhaps, made all that happened to the family thereafter possible. Sir Henry was held prisoner in the Tower of London for two years (1483–1485) because of his Yorkist sympathies and, according to family tradition, might well have starved to death but for a cat which he befriended or which – cats being cats – befriended him and caught pigeons and brought them to him in his cell. True or not, Sir Henry certainly did survive and was released by Henry VII in time to become a Privy Councillor and guardian of the King's son.

One of Kent's most illustrious sons was Sir Philip Sidney, who was born in 1554 at Penshurst Place, the already ancient ancestral home of his distinguished family. He grew up to be one of those favourites of fortune that emerge once in a while to shine in their own time and to leave an afterglow that mellows but never dims.

After a distinguished academic life, he travelled a great deal before he settled down in England to become one of the most successful courtiers of his day, and a favourite of Queen Elizabeth I. When he thought seriously of joining Sir Francis Drake's second expedition to the West Indies in 1585, the Queen expressly forbade him to do any such thing 'lest we should lose the jewel of our dominions'.

To take his mind off the disappointment, Elizabeth appointed Sidney Governor of Flushing, and he led English and Dutch troops in a number of engagements against the Spanish.

It was after the Battle of Zutphen in September 1586, in which he took a bullet in the left thigh and had to be carried from the field, that he spoke the words that have been far better remembered than any of his more literary compositions. Thirsty because he had lost a great deal of blood, he called for a drink, but before tasting it he offered it to another wounded soldier who was obviously dying, saying: 'Thy necessity is yet greater than mine.'

As it turned out, the comparative necessity was a matter of time only. Sidney died twenty-five days later at Arnhem aged thirty-two, in the arms of his wife. Despite the Dutch wish to bury him in their country, he was brought back to England and buried in old St Paul's, where his tomb was destroyed in the Great Fire in 1666.

A contemporary of Sir Philip's, in the sense that they shared some part of the sixteenth century although they certainly never met, was an Elizabethan sea-dog whose contribution to Kentish lore was, in fact, rather less significant than his place in the lore of Japan.

He was Will Adams, who was born in Gillingham in 1564 and learned his seafaring as an apprentice to a London shipbuilder. By the time he was twenty-four, he was master of a 120-ton fleet transport vessel ferrying food and arms out to Drake's ships where they waited in the Channel for the Spanish Armada to arrive.

He was a good seaman, and he spoke both Dutch and Portuguese, so when a group of Dutch merchants went talent-spotting for someone to pilot one of five ships they planned to send to the Far East, they came to Will Adams.

It meant leaving his wife, Mary, and their child, Deliverance, but the expedition offered adventure and better rewards than the routine trading voyages he was used to, so off he went down the Thames in June 1598 to join the Dutch ships at Rotterdam, expecting to be away three or four years.

In fact, he never returned. After a voyage that fulfilled every expectation he had ever harboured of adventure, Adams' ship was eventually the only one of the little fleet to reach Japan, in April 1600. There they were held as something between honoured guests – Will Adams was, in fact, the first Englishman to set foot on Japanese soil – and suspected intruders. But Adams managed to strike up a good relationship with the Shogun and agreed to teach the Japanese the art and craft of making European-style seagoing vessels.

He became a prosperous trader in Tokyo and a wealthy landowning nobleman. He married a local girl and raised a family before he died in May 1620, after which Japan became almost completely isolated from European traders until 1853, when Commodore Perry took American warships there to urge the country back into world trade. It probably seemed a good idea at the time!

Will Adams might never have survived in the loreful memory of his native Gillingham if an Englishman named James Walter had not rediscovered the lost Adams family tombs in 1872 and reawakened interest, both here and in Japan, in the Elizabethan seaman who was hailed as the father of the Japanese navy. The Japanese even wanted to make him a Shinto saint, but the best his old home town in Kent ever did for him was to build a rather unlovely memorial clock tower in 1934 which has become a 'must' for all Japanese visitors to the Medway Towns.

In the Thames-side town of Gravesend, American visitors are equally diligent about taking their cameras to the statue of a movingly serene-looking Red Indian girl. This is the statue of Princess Pocahontas, the first native American visitor to England. Her niche in Kentish lore is a small one; it was chipped out by her chance death aboard the ship that was taking her home, and by the local claim that she was, in fact, buried in St George's Church there.

There is some doubt about that, and the matter is unlikely to be resolved now. The church was burned down in 1727, and although it was rebuilt on the same site in 1731, records were lost in the fire so that the site of the grave is now unknown.

Still, in her day she was a great celebrity, and the story of how she came to be in England at all – while not necessarily true in every particular as commonly told – was a romantic one which has survived more than 350 years during which much else that is much more certain about her has been all but forgotten.

Pocahontas was an Indian princess in Virginia when an expeditionary group of settlers arrived in what is now Jamestown in 1607. One of the leaders of the group was Captain John Smith, a rough, tough adventurer, it seems, who was prepared to be peaceful towards the Indians but ready to exploit them if he could, too.

The paramount chief of the region was Powhatan, whose daughter Pocahontas was, and she seems to have fallen pretty heavily for the bearded Englishman when he finally fell victim to an Indian war party and was taken to Powhatan. When Smith was sentenced to die by having his brains hammered out with stone tomahawks, and was trussed up and thrown down onto a big stone brought to the chief's feet for the purpose, little Pocahontas threw herself upon the Englishman, shielding him from the upraised weapons of his executioners.

Taking advantage of local custom, she claimed him as her man, which made him a member of the chief's family and saved his life. As it happened, it was not the first time Smith had had his life saved, so it was not, perhaps, the gratitude-demanding novelty for him that it might have been for others. Although by no means oblivious of the charms of the little near-naked native girl, and more than willing to accept her life-saving gesture, he saw no reason to consider himself bound to her to anything like the extent she clearly enough felt herself to be bound to him.

At the first opportunity that presented itself he went back to the Jamestown settlement, with no intention of returning to Pocahontas. The girl followed him and as a result became to some extent familiar with English people and English ways, but she did not stay with him. Smith became something of a legend among the Indians for his travels through their country, and at last Powhatan, despite the kinship, plotted to kill him. During one of his visits, the chief prepared a feast for the Englishman and his party, intending to have them all killed while they ate. But Pocahontas warned them, and they escaped.

At last Smith returned to England, leaving the Indian girl, now in her early teens, with her own people. Word went around that he had died aboard the ship, and it seemed that the Pocahontas legend might never come to England at all.

But the Jamestown settlement prospered after some tragic early setbacks, and more settlers arrived, among them a widower called John Rolfe. Pocahontas found herself more and more attracted to the ways of the Englishmen and visited the town again. This time she was taken hostage for the good behaviour of Powhatan, and she lived with the family of Sir Thomas Gates, where she learned to dress and behave in the English fashion.

It was during this period of captivity/adoption that she met Rolfe and taught him how to grow tobacco. For a time she worked alongside him in his fields and eventually married him in Jamestown and bore him a son. In 1616 she and Rolfe and their baby son came to England. It was a dream come true for Pocahontas, who had learned about London from Smith and his friends long before she met Rolfe, although when she reached this promised land at last it must have been something of a disappointment to her.

Nevertheless, she met Queen Anne and King James I, and she attended fashionable balls and other occasions and had her portrait painted. When she was ill, the Queen sent her own doctor to tend her.

She met Smith again, too. He was not the fine, swaggering figure of authority in his own country that he had been in hers, and the meeting must have been a disillusionment. There seems to have been no reawakening of the old love she had felt for him when she saved his life, at any rate, and soon after that she and Rolfe prepared to leave England to return to the American colony.

But before they sailed Pocahontas fell sick again. The robust little savage who had run naked through the Virginian woods, frolicked like an otter in icy streams and slept rough in wintertime without coming to any harm had no defences against the diseases with which London was riddled. Before the ship left the Thames, Pocahontas died, and, to take what must necessarily be largely if not essentially legend to its customary conclusion, she was buried in St George's Church, Gravesend, in March 1617.

While Pocahontas was growing up in Virginia, England was going through one of its periodic times of political turmoil, and in 1605 the infamous Gunpowder Plot was hatched with the object of blowing up the King and the Houses of Parliament and all the members on the one occasion of the year when it was most likely to be possible to do that with just one explosion, the State Opening of Parliament.

As every Englishman knows, of course, the plot was discovered before the fuses were lit, and the King and Parliament survived. But quite how the plot was foiled, or by whom, has never been wholly satisfactorily explained – except by those who accept the Kentish legend that it was thanks to Dame Dorothy Selby of Ightham Mote, near Sevenoaks.

Today Ightham Mote is one of the finest moated houses in England, owned by an American and promised to the National Trust after his lifetime. It is open to the public sometimes, and visitors are always shown the portrait of Dame Dorothy and told the story of how she gave the warning that led to the plot being discovered and thwarted.

But there is a good deal of doubt about whether or not it really was Dame Dorothy, and, indeed, about how she did it – if she did.

The Selby family owned Ightham Mote for almost three hundred years, and the first two members of the family to own it were both called William, uncle and nephew. Dame Dorothy was wife of the second William. She enjoyed a reputation for fine needlework, which is mentioned in the inscription on her monument in Ightham church. She was no obscure countrywoman, but a woman with connections at Court both on her own account and, of course, on her husband's too. She was, in fact, at one time lady-in-waiting to Elizabeth I.

So it is certainly by no means impossible that she did pick up a hint or even became privy to more exact knowledge about the plotters' plans.

However it was, the story tells that she learned about the plot and sent an unsigned letter to her cousin, Lord Mounteagle, warning him to stay away from the Opening of Parliament that year, without saying why. Lord Mounteagle, however, claimed to recognize the handwriting of his cousin Dorothy and put in hand the inquiries that ultimately led to the arrest of the plotters.

There is nothing merely legendary about the fact that, when the Great Hall of Ightham Mote was panelled in 1872, a blocked-up cupboard was uncovered in which was seated a female skeleton. But we are back in the realms of local lore with the assumption that the old bones were those of Dame Dorothy, who, incidentally, is said to haunt the old house in the spectral shape of a mysterious Grey Lady.

And so the abiding lore of Kent threads together age after age of the county's eventful past.

In 1676 a highwayman robbed a traveller on infamous Gad's Hill, at Higham near Rochester, at four o'clock one morning, and immediately took horse to York, where he played a game of bowls at a quarter to eight that same evening in order to establish for himself an alibi to prove he could not have been responsible for the robbery in Kent nearly sixteen hours before. The ride, which was barely credible in its time, was the origin of the national legend of Dick Turpin's ride on his horse, Black Bess.

Did it really happen? Never question it in Kent! Dick Turpin may indeed have been a highwayman, but every Kentish Man knows that it was the local man who made the ride and that the man who lost the kudos for it to the lesser rogue from out of the shires was, in truth, Kent's own Swift Nick.

In Tunbridge Wells, the most widely known fragment of local lore is the old story about how the town came by its most magnetic tourist trap, the Pantiles. This was originally one of the famous Walks, where fashionable visitors to the spa took their exercise between prescribed treatments of drinking or bathing in the local mineral spring water and enjoying the other delights of the town.

One of those visitors was Princess – later Queen – Anne. In 1698 she gave £100 to have the Upper Walk paved. There is some doubt (in history, if not in lore) about whether the gift was prompted by the misfortune of her son, the young Duke of Gloucester, who is supposed to have tripped on the unevenness of the ground and, falling, cut his knee. But it is generally agreed that, when the Queen returned to the Wells the following year and found that her money had not been spent as she had directed, she left in a huff and never returned, although the paving, with the now famous pantiles, was carried out soon after.

Today, the Pantiles survive in name only, the real thing having been replaced by more conventional paving in 1793, but some of the old buildings and a hint or two of the old style remain.

One of the great characters of Tunbridge Wells was Belle Causey, 'governess' of the town from 1724 to 1734. She was, by all accounts, a fine, large woman with a commanding personality, who directed the company of visitors in all the pleasures and amusements of this 'valley of pleasure and sink of iniquity', and to raise money to provide the entertainments she used to stand outside the chapel and spread her apron to solicit contributions from the congregation.

Another of her ploys was to issue special invitations to wealthy strangers to buy themselves into favour by hosting public breakfasts and tea-parties.

Belle was paid two guineas a day for conducting a gaming room, and she spent it all on hospitality. If ever any was left over, she gave it away to the local poor, and so was equally beloved of rich and poor. It was not until after she died that Richard (Beau) Nash arrived in Tunbridge Wells and declared himself Master of Ceremonies. Under his guidance the town's reputation was both enhanced and purified, at least to some extent, although well into old age he retained the company if not the affections of his mistress of many years, the delightfully named Juliana Papjoy.

With a few notable exceptions, Kent had not contributed a particularly large number of sporting greats. Quite why that should be is not easy to explain, yet it has to be acknowledged that it is so.

One of the exceptions, though, very nearly made up for all the shortcomings on his own. He was the legendary Alfred Mynn – 'Mighty Mynn' as he was known to cricketing enthusiasts 150 years ago: the Lion of Kent. Mynn was born on 19 January 1807 near Goudhurst, and his sporting instincts were inherited from several generations of a family that had had a reputation for exceptional heights and strength. Alfred grew to top six feet and weighed a well-proportioned eighteen stone.

His enthusiasm for cricket seems to have resulted from a family move to Harrietsham, on the Ashford side of Maidstone, in 1825. The village happened, at the time, to have one of the best cricket clubs in Kent, and soon Mynn was completely hooked on the game.

He became a good batsman and a first-rate bowler, and in 1832 he made his name as a single-wicket player by defeating the Kent champion, a man called Hills, and earning for himself the title of Lion of Kent.

For the next twenty years after that, the name of Alfred Mynn was a famous one. He first played at Lords in 1832, and he took part in all the important matches of his time, including twenty Gentlemen v Players matches. He played regularly for Kent until 1854, and less regularly until 1860, not only against other counties but also All England teams which Kent beat a number of times.

In fact, during Mynn's career, largely thanks to his own performances, Kent became the most famous and the most successful cricketing county in England.

Once, in 1836, Mynn batted for several hours with a painfully injured leg during a North v South match at Leicester, only retiring when his score reached 125. He had to be taken to St Bartholomew's Hospital in London, where doctors thought they might have to amputate the leg, but his great strength and superb physical fitness saw him through, and he was out of hospital, with both feet on the ground again, in two months.

In 1836 he scored 283 runs in four successive innings and was not out in two of them. When he played in the first Canterbury Cricket Week Kent v England game in 1842, he defended his wicket for most of one day.

He was a member of the All England XI for eight years, playing for the last time at Lords in 1854, at the Oval in 1858 and for Kent (v Middlesex) in 1856.

Throughout his career, Mynn neglected practically everything for his sport and was brought close to poverty by it. But he was married, to the daughter of a Lenham doctor, and they had seven children.

He lived the last years of his life at Thurnham, a little village at the foot of the Maidstone side of the North Downs, although he actually died in London, on 1 November 1861, aged fifty-four. His body was brought home to the village, where he was buried in the churchyard with military honours, as befitted a member of the Leeds and Hollingbourne Volunteers.

Today Thurnham is hardly distinguishable from the nearby Maidstone suburb of Bearsted where the village green still remembers Mynn very well. On the green is a fine village sign which shows Mighty Mynn at the wicket there, top-hatted and perhaps flexing his muscular shoulders for that hit that is equally part of cricketing, Mynn and Bearsted lore: the day he lifted the ball from the wicket in the middle of the green, across the road, over some brewery buildings and gardens and into a field beyond them. A truly once-in-a-lifetime hit that deserves to be remembered among the most abiding lore of Kent.

4

Lore of the Land

In the earliest days of man's settlement in Kent, much of the area was heavily forested, and so the settlers, who were, after all, farmers, made their homes in the more open grazing lands of East and North Kent. That is why much of the lore of the county is associated with these parts rather than with the comparatively much younger settlements of South and West Kent.

Thanet, for example, where the Saxon homesteaders first got their taste for the good life that Britain offered, is particularly well endowed with lore of all kinds.

Take the story of King Egbert who, in the seventh century, had his palace at Eastry, today a picturesque but otherwise fairly insignificant village to the south of Sandwich, but then the capital of the Kentish kingdom, no less.

Egbert, it is said, feared that he might be challenged for his throne by either or both of two young cousins, and so he plotted with one of his henchmen, a fellow called Thunor, to murder them. The deed was duly done, and the more certainly to hide all traces of the crime, the bodies were buried under the King's own throne, where, it was confidently supposed, nobody would search for them.

But in fact – well, in lore at any rate – a miraculous beam of light shafted down upon the very spot, drawing attention to it and prompting a search which discovered the bodies and revealed the crime.

The King, obliged by Saxon law to pay compensation to the dead boys' relatives, agreed with their sister Ermenburga, Queen of Northumbria and great-granddaughter of Ethelbert, Kent's first Christian King, that he would grant her land upon which to build an abbey. The agreement was that the Queen should release a pet deer and that all the land it covered in a single day's coursing should be hers.

Well, the deer covered several hundred acres during the day, but the King kept his side of the bargain, and Ermenburga duly built her abbey. Some versions of the story say she chose as the site for the building the spot where the hind finally stopped running. Others that she settled upon suitable land near where her own ancestors, Hengist and Horsa, had landed in 449, and where St Augustine and his forty monks had stepped ashore in 597 to begin the mission that led to the baptism of her royal ancestor.

Whichever it was, Ermenburga changed her name to Domneva and became the first head of her new monastery, which later gave its name to the village which grew up around it and is still, today, the largest of the Thanet parishes, Minster.

A rather nice – or, I suppose rather nasty; certainly dramatic – twist to the story tells how the murderer, Thunor, counselled his King not to enter into the somewhat open-ended agreement with the Mercian Queen, but had the ground taken from under his feet – and not just in a manner of speaking, either – when the earth opened up beneath him and swallowed him up, pretty conclusively discrediting him as a counsellor.

Then there is the apparently immortal story of the golden statue of Odin which, lorefully, is buried somewhere near Dover. As is the case with most lore, there are variations on the main theme, but there are those alive today who, in the absence of any evidence that it was ever discovered, are prepared to believe that the long-lost Saxon treasure is still waiting to be found, in defiance of any real evidence that it ever existed in the first place.

No one really knows where to start looking for it, though, and would-be treasure-hunters are pretty equally divided in believing that the best clues are in local place-names, of which Guilton (gelt – that is, gold – town?) and Woodnesborough (Woden's borough?) are probably top contenders.

It's a bit like the story of the Colossus of Richborough. Excavators of the Roman fortress there have unearthed massive foundations thirty feet deep and cross-shaped, and although no one knows for certain what was on top of this immense underpinning, its size and shape have suggested to some experts that it was probably some sort of statue, or possibly a triumphal arch, perhaps erected to commemorate the conquest of Britain by the Romans.

It used to be quite confidently supposed that there was under or even in the foundations a treasure chamber full of who-knew-what fabulous treasures, but although the belief has never been

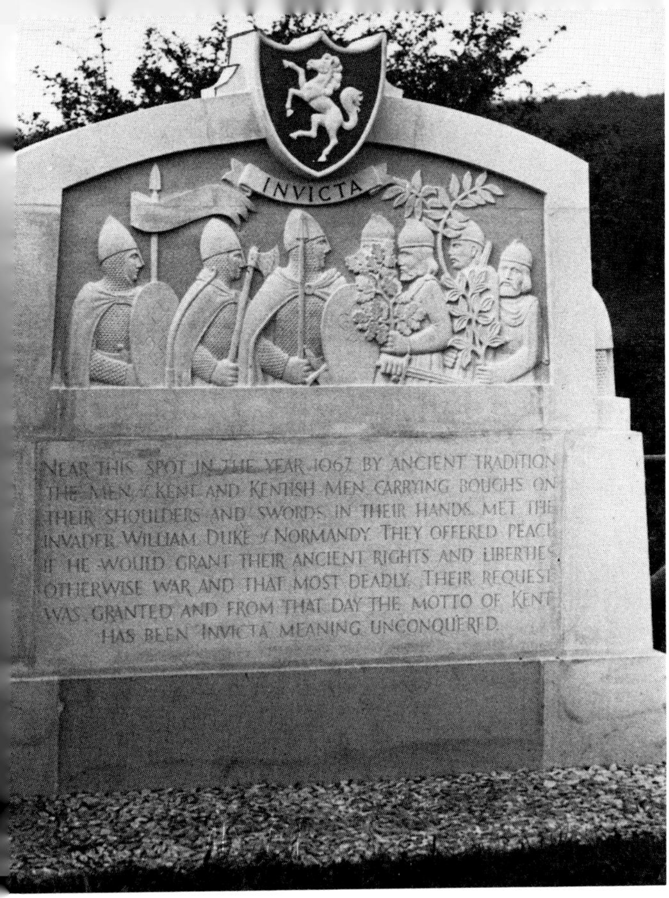
INVICTA
NEAR THIS SPOT IN THE YEAR 1067 BY ANCIENT TRADITION
THE MEN OF KENT AND KENTISH MEN CARRYING BOUGHS ON
THEIR SHOULDERS AND SWORDS IN THEIR HANDS MET THE
INVADER WILLIAM DUKE OF NORMANDY THEY OFFERED PEACE
IF HE WOULD GRANT THEIR ANCIENT RIGHTS AND LIBERTIES
OTHERWISE WAR AND THAT MOST DEADLY. THEIR REQUEST
WAS GRANTED AND FROM THAT DAY THE MOTTO OF KENT
HAS BEEN INVICTA MEANING UNCONQUERED

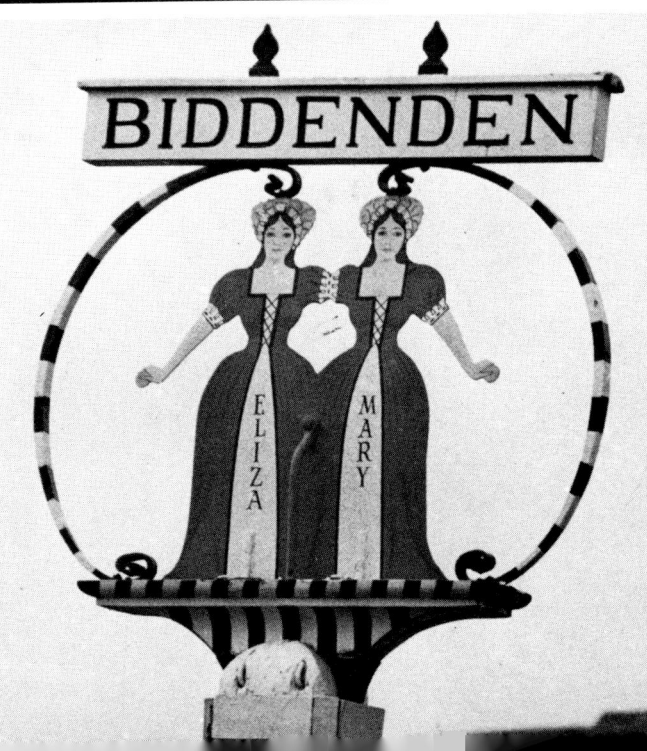

The Invicta Memorial on the traditional spot where Kentish Men and Men of Kent met William the Conqueror to demand continuation of ancient rights

BIDDENDEN
ELIZA
MARY

Biddenden Maids Eliza and Mary Chulkhurst are commemorated on the village sign

The reputed tomb of Richard Plantagenet in the ruins of St Mary's Church, Eastwell

Below left: Gillingham remembers its links with Japan with this memorial to local seafarer Will Adams

Below right: The statue of Pocahontas in Gravesend keeps alive the story of the Indian princess who died there

The tiles that gave 'The Pantiles' at Tunbridge Wells its name are gone, but the tale of their origin is still told

The village sign at Bearsted commemorates the legendary Kent cricketer Alfred Mynn, 'Lion of Kent'

The Countless Stones, Aylesford—does the Devil himself guard the secret of their number?

Prehistoric Kit's Coty at Aylesford, the legendary tomb of Catigern, Prince of Kent

The beauty of ballerina Gianetta Baccelli, preserved in this stone figure at Knole, Sevenoaks, is also enshrined in Kentish lore

The incredible Shell Grotto at Margate—prehistoric mystery or nineteenth-century folly?

The tower of St Mildred's Church at Tenterden, lorefully
accused of being the cause of the Goodwin Sands

The Headcorn Oak,
perhaps more than
a thousand years old, is
alive and lore-supporting
still

The Goodwin Sands—
sometimes friend, often
foe, but what is the truth
about their origins?

St Augustine's Cross at Ebbsfleet, Isle of Thanet, marks the spot where, traditionally, St Augustine met King Ethelbert of Kent in AD 597

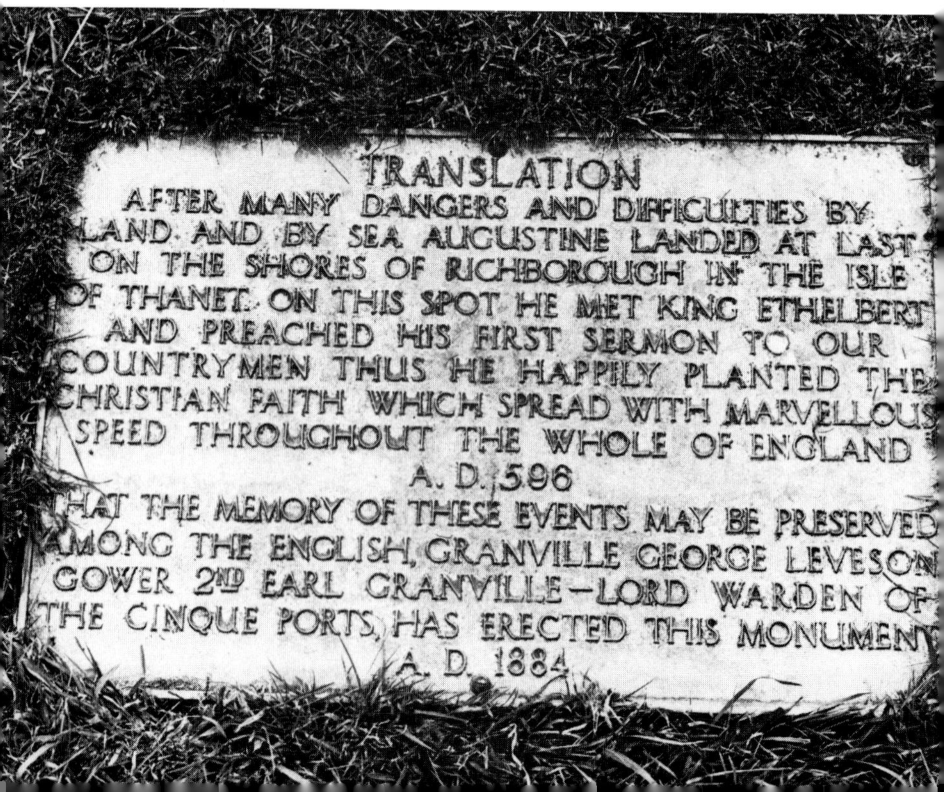

A translation of the inscription on St Augustine's Cross

TRANSLATION

AFTER MANY DANGERS AND DIFFICULTIES BY LAND AND BY SEA AUGUSTINE LANDED AT LAST ON THE SHORES OF RICHBOROUGH IN THE ISLE OF THANET. ON THIS SPOT HE MET KING ETHELBERT AND PREACHED HIS FIRST SERMON TO OUR COUNTRYMEN THUS HE HAPPILY PLANTED THE CHRISTIAN FAITH WHICH SPREAD WITH MARVELLOUS SPEED THROUGHOUT THE WHOLE OF ENGLAND
A.D. 596
THAT THE MEMORY OF THESE EVENTS MAY BE PRESERVED AMONG THE ENGLISH, GRANVILLE GEORGE LEVESON GOWER 2ND EARL GRANVILLE — LORD WARDEN OF THE CINQUE PORTS, HAS ERECTED THIS MONUMENT
A.D. 1884

exactly disproved, no trace of any such thing has so far come to light.

Further west along the North Kent coastal strip a similarly loreful legend clings to the little village of Tonge, near Teynham, which once boasted a castle but today is better known for the reproduction antiques and original handicrafts on sale at Tonge Mill.

Of Tonge it is said that, in the days when the Jutes were beginning to covet the good land beyond the Isle of Thanet which their hosts had given them in exchange for a promise of help to defend the kingdom against the raids of hostile northerners, King Vortigern of Kent met Hengist, the Jute chieftain, and offered him as much land as he could cover with a single ox hide.

No doubt he thought he wasn't going to lose more than a very small patch, but the wily Jute accepted the offer and had an ox hide prepared and cut into thongs (hence the name of the village) which he laid end to end round an area of land equivalent to many 'hides', the old English land measure.

As a matter of fact, Judith Glover, in her book *The Place Names of Kent*, reckons the name more likely derived from a tongue of land, which is to say a strip protruding into a neighbouring area. We might argue that, the two are by no means mutually eliminating, because the 'thonged' land might very well have created a 'tongue' of land within Mrs Glover's meaning of the term.

One of the county's several prehistoric sites lies just across the River Stour from Chilham. It is a long barrow, now heavily overgrown and not particularly easy to identify, known as Jul-liberries Grave. It was almost certainly the work of the same race that built parts of Stonehenge and other prehistoric stonework throughout Britain, but the name of the original occupant is long lost if it was ever recorded. Lore, but nothing else, sometimes suggests that the name is a corruption of Julius Laberius, one of Julius Caesar's tribunes killed in a battle near Chilham during Caesar's invasion in 54 BC.

Well, it may be at that, although the 'grave' was certainly there long before the Romans went into their coming, seeing and conquering routine.

Still among the ancient stones of Kent, the village of Chidding-stone, near Edenbridge in West Kent, is said to take its name from the local lump of sandstone which, according to lore, once featured in druidical rites. There is absolutely no real evidence that that is so, of course, but then lore, unlike law, is at its strongest when the evidence is weakest.

Come to that, there isn't a lot more substance in the parallel conviction that the stone was once the Chiding Stone to which local scolds were brought to be punished.

Back on the other side of the county, near Aylesford village, north of Maidstone, there is a collection of great stones lying tumbled around a tree which has apparently grown up through them. They are known locally as Little (sometimes Lower) Kit's Coty or, to some, the Countless Stones. There is, as a matter of fact, a certain confusion about just what the stones are called, because there is another group of Countless Stones, and whether the following story properly attaches to one or both groups, or whether time has confused the identity of the original Countless Stones, I do not know. Either way, however, the story that clings to them is certainly part of Kentish lore.

It seems that the idea grew up that it was not possible to count the stones because of the way they lay, and a local baker hit upon what he deemed to be a novel way of disproving that reputation by arriving at an indisputable total.

Taking a basket of penny loaves with him, he went to the stones and began to count them. To make sure he didn't miss one, or count one twice, he placed a loaf on each as he numbered it. But before his task was finished, he found that the loaves were disappearing as fast as he took his eyes off them. The discovery was enough to persuade him that the number of the stones was a secret closely guarded by the Devil himself, and the baker abandoned his task and the loaves, and left the stones countless as ever.

Unfortunately, that particular legend is one of those that travel rather well so that it, or one very like it, is told of similar groups of so-called countless stones all over Britain, and there is none to say now where or of which group it was first told.

The most famous of all Kent's old stones is, of course, Kit's Coty itself, standing starkly within its iron fence in a hillside field above Aylesford village. The three great upright slabs capped by a fourth have been said by some experts to be an older construction than Stonehenge, and as recently as two hundred years ago the stones were still a discernible part of a two-hundred-foot-long barrow or burial chamber.

Since then, the soil has eroded away, leaving the stones as we see them now. Like Julliberries Grave near Chilham, it certainly predates anyone of whom history has kept any note, yet there have been attempts to identify this as the mausoleum of the Celtic Prince Catigern (son of that Vortigern who was outwitted by the Jutes at Tonge), who, according to lore, was killed in the great Battle of Aylesford in 455.

It is lore, too, that tells us that Catigern and Horsa the Jute, brother of Hengist, engaged in single combat on the Aylesford battlefield and killed each other. It is as near certain as these things ever can be that the long barrow that once covered the Kit's Coty stones was heaped up several thousand years before that fatal day in 455, but of course that does not necessarily invalidate the rest of the story, nor mean that the barrow was never opened up and used to entomb the princely corpse.

Apart from the origins of the stones themselves, there have been several explanations suggested for the name of the structure. Some are more fanciful than others. Personally, I like the idea of a certain young Christopher being sent up onto the bleak hillside to look after sheep and using the old stones for a shelter against the weather. Certainly, the formation, with its capped uprights, could be called a coty (cottage) by anyone not too particular about the precision of language – or by a boy with an imaginative hankering for home comforts up there on the hillside.

If Horsa was in fact killed at the same time as Catigern, is there no loreful monument to him? Well, yes, there is, also at Aylesford. It is a heap of stones known as 'The Horsted' – far less impressive than Kit's Coty. On the one hand, that alone might not make its claim to be the grave of a rebellious foreign mercenary too improbable. It might, after all, be expected that the native prince would have the grander tomb.

On the other hand, though, it was the Jutes who won the battle and finally drove the Celts out of all the best bits of Kent if not out of the county altogether, which might suggest that their hero could have expected to have been the more grandly remembered. However . . .

Back in that lore-full area east of Canterbury, beneath a pond near the village church at Preston, between Sandwich and Canterbury, is said to await excavation the remains of a palace once owned by Juliana de Leybourne, so-called Infanta (Princess) of Kent. She was one of the richest of mid-fourteenth-century

Kentish landowners, but the title carried no implications of royal descent.

Another famous lady who has tangled with the lore since her death is remembered at Westenhanger (near Hythe), where two towers, one round and the other square, are linked by the remnants of an old wall. One of the towers is reputed to be the remains of the famous bower of the equally famous Fair Rosamund, mistress of Henry II.

Upholders of the lore are well advised not to delve too deeply into history for fear of spoiling a good yarn with the truth, and history's ideas about where Rosamund's bower was do not, I fear, favour Kent. Nevertheless, Westenhanger's claim is a persistent one.

Buildings of all kinds hug their own lore to themselves, sometimes implicating people, though not always.

The Dering windows at Pluckley, for instance, owe their existence to the local family. No reasonably observant visitor to the village could fail to notice the way all the older cottages there seem to be looking back at the world with perpetually raised eyebrows. Some visitors might think there was nothing very questionable about that, although the visible world around Pluckley is, perhaps, less deserving of raised eyebrows than a great many other parts.

The windows all have the same round-topped design, not quite unique to the locality, to be sure, but certainly there are more of them, even today, in the parish than anywhere else in Kent.

That is because they were installed in every home on the fifty-thousand-acre Dering estate on the orders of the nineteenth-century squire Sir Edward Cholmeley Dering, who deemed such windows, with their white-painted outer arch and frame, to be lucky.

He came to that conclusion when he found out about his ancestor, the first baronet, a political fence-sitter during the Civil War, a time when Roundheads and Cavaliers were equally prone to take a dim view of any kind of divided loyalty.

As a result, the squire of Pluckley finally found himself without friends in both camps and actually had to run for his life. He escaped from his own home through a window with the now familiar rounded top, and although the fugitive himself showed no special gratitude, his successor, Sir Edward Cholmeley, made the windows a memorial throughout the ancestral estate.

Of Knole House at Sevenoaks, one of the stateliest of all Kent's stately homes, it is said that there were seven courtyards, representing the days of the week, 52 staircases for the number of weeks in a year, and 365 rooms, one for each day of the year. The numbers have become part of the lore of Knole, but in her book *Knole and the Sackvilles*, Vita Sackville-West admitted that she had been unable to verify this 'old conceit'.

Less of an old conceit, though, is Shelley's Tower, one of the turrets flanking Bourchier's Gateway at Knole. The gateway was named after the fifteenth-century archbishop who owned Knole and who added the gateway and other features. But who, then, was the Shelley after whom the tower was named?

Well, it is said that the name was bequeathed to us by eighteenth-century Knole servants whose less than meticulous elocution derived it from the Italian pronunciation of Baccelli.

If that does little to clarify the mystery, it can only be because you have never been to Knole and been instantly and unforgettably impressed with the lovely reclining nude statue of Gianetta Baccelli.

La Baccelli was a ballet dancer who captivated John Sackville, third Duke of Dorset and owner of Knole in the second half of the eighteenth century, while he was Ambassador in Paris. He brought her back to Knole with him and installed her in a suite of her own over the Bourchier Gatehouse reached by a staircase in the little tower, where she remained as his mistress for several years. Today, the tower and the statue remain to link history and lore *in memoriam* of a beautiful friendship of two hundred years ago.

A very different structure from the romantic little Shelley's Tower at Knole is the great slabby tower of St Mildred's Church at Tenterden. But it, too, has had its brush with the lore.

At Tenterden they do say it was the cause of the infamous Goodwin Sands, the fearful 'shippe swallower' some four miles off the Kent coast which has, down the years, sucked so many vessels of all sizes into its depths, and which has gathered in quite a substantial body of lore of its own in the process.

There are several versions of how the one-time Isle of Lomea was flooded and became the Sands. One of them claims that a certain abbot of St Augustine's at Canterbury, who owned land on Lomea, was also rector of Tenterden and that, at a time when he should have been spending money on stone with which to improve the island's decaying sea defences, the Abbot chose instead to spend the money on stone for improvements to his church at Tenterden.

One of those improvements, so the story goes, was the great tower, with the result that the Lomea sea wall was breached, the land was flooded and was never again reclaimed. What had been fertile acres of offshore farmland became one of the most notoriously treacherous sandbanks in the world.

A more popular version of what is clearly the same legend blames the Saxon Earl Godwin, Earl of Kent and father of that King Harold who lost his eye and his crown to William the Conqueror at Hastings in 1066. That version claims that Lomea was Godwin's own land, which he had to leave in order to fight the Danes in another part of the county. During one of his battles, he found himself cut off and trapped by a Danish force in the Weald, and it looked as though the Saxon was never going to see Lomea again.

Desperately, he made a vow that, if the Blessed Virgin Mary would only return him safely home, he would build a steeple on Tenterden church as a thanks-offering. Well, whether or not it was by divine intervention, Godwin did escape his enemies and did return to Lomea where, in the excitement of his homecoming and one thing and another, he promptly forgot all about his vow. The reminder was swift and allowed no second chance. A great storm breached the sea defences, flooded the land and made it into the sandbank we know today.

Nice enough stories, both of them but, as historians are all too eager to point out, almost certainly not true, because it seems most likely that the Goodwin Sands have been as they are today for much longer than the nine hundred years or so that would take in Earl Godwin's day. Even if they had not, the story about the imprudent Abbot would still be untrue. Tenterden church did not have a tower until the sixteenth century.

A nice example of how lore attaches itself to buildings is provided by Chilham Castle, where it is said that, if the herons do not return to the heronry there by St Valentine's Day (14 February) each year, disaster will befall the castle towers. Whether or not the old belief has ever been put to the test is one of those things that lore frequently glosses over.

Lore, like law, quite often becomes involved with the underworld, and has done in a number of parts of Kent.

The old Saxon capital of Kent, Eastry near Sandwich, has earned mention already, with a hint then that there might be more lore beneath the surface. When the King's henchman, Thunor, was swallowed up by the earth for his part in the murder of the King's young cousins, he was, perhaps, not so much the victim of retribution from above as of lack of support from below.

Today, Eastry Court claims to stand on the site of the one-time palace of the Kentish kings – itself a more loreful than historical claim – but beneath the house there is still part of what remains of what may once have been the most extensive labyrinth of tunnels, passages and caverns in the county.

Some say this elaborate underground network was once used for mysterious prehistoric rites and rituals; others that it is what remains of successive generations of treasure-hunters' excavations, presumably seeking that elusive golden Odin.

But it is inconceivable that such a labyrinth should exist without attracting the interest of the lore in a more historically probable guise than that. Sure enough, the Eastry labyrinth is said to be where Archbishop Thomas Becket hid in the days immediately before he sailed from Sandwich into exile in France in 1164. Furthermore, it is said that he used the tunnels to gain secret access to Eastry's church of St Mary the Virgin to hear Mass and to give his archiepiscopal blessing to the congregation from a secret chamber (now, unhappily for history but much to the advantage of lore, lost) without anyone, even the priest in charge, knowing he was there.

There are other passages and caves and labyrinths in Kent, too. Many of them are too small or too modern or just too modest altogether to have attracted the attentions of the lore-makers. Some claim links with the smugglers who operated all over Kent for centuries, and no doubt those claims are true in at least some cases, although most of the caves probably existed long before they were pressed into service as caches for illicit trade goods.

Another very extensive labyrinth is at Chislehurst, where there is a Map Room with a wall plan showing the layout of the caves. It looks just like a town map. Some of the caves and tunnels were apparently dug by Saxons, some by Romans. Some are almost certainly prehistoric and are believed by some people to have once been a secret Druids' College. For sure, during World War II they were used as air-raid shelters.

At Leybourne, near Maidstone, there is said to be an underground passageway, the route and destination of which once so intrigued two investigators that they hit upon a scheme for clearing up the mystery once and for all. While one of them went into the tunnel playing a fiddle as he walked along in the subterranean darkness, the other followed the sound of the fiddle on the surface.

All went well until, in the middle of a wood (ever afterwards known as Fiddler's Copse), the sound of the fiddling stopped abruptly, and the player was never seen again.

In fact, this is another of those stories, like that of the baker and the countless stones, that seems to have travelled all over the country. Sometimes it was a fiddler that ventured into the tunnel; sometimes a drummer or a flautist. In Scotland, naturally, there was an intrepid piper. All vanished mysteriously, leaving the full extent and direction of the tunnel unresolved.

Not, of course, that that necessarily means that none or, for that matter, any of the stories is true. It is just that element of 'surely not – and yet . . .' that makes lore so much more fascinating even than history itself.

The Hollingbourne labyrinth, on the opposite side of Maidstone from Leybourne, seems to have steered clear of the lore. If ever fantastic legends were born in its sandy passageways, they have not survived into modern times. The labyrinth was discovered in the 1890s when a hunted fox went to earth in an overgrown entrance, and subsequent explorers found flint tools there, which led them to speculate that the caves were used by prehistoric residents. They were opened to the public in 1930 by a man who owned the Caves café there, but they were closed fourteen years later, and although one amateur explorer did once volunteer to spend a fortnight underground mapping the full extent of the caves and passages, his offer was never accepted, and the labyrinth was, for the most part, quietly forgotten about.

There is some good reason to suppose that the caves were, in fact, dug no earlier than in about 1850 to provide sand for the glass that went into the building of the Crystal Palace, though whether sand was then merely taken from existing caves is not clear. In any case, the mystery may never now be solved, for the whole hill into which the caves were burrowed was bulldozed away when the eastern end of the M20 Maidstone bypass was built.

The Margate grotto is quite different. This curiosity, of which it has been said that, if it existed anywhere but at Margate, it would certainly have been acknowledged as one of the wonders of the world, was thrust into the nineteenth century when the son of a Dane Hill landowner dug his spade into what he supposed was an old well shaft and discovered a passageway cut into the chalk, leading to a rectangular chamber.

Other passages and chambers were discovered later, and all were found to be covered with millions of small shells laid into the walls in intricate designs and symbols.

Named 'The Grotto', the discovery was commercialized to such an extent that gas lighting installed for the benefit of visitors ruined the subtlety of the colours of the shells. Nonetheless, it is still a thing of wonder, and of mystery, too, because experts differ about why or when or by whom the mosaic of pearly pinks and blues and yellows was created. Some historians have dismissed it as an eighteenth-century folly created by some unknown eccentric. But what eccentricity! The cost in labour and time would have been considerable for one man, and if he employed help, the financial cost would have been greater still.

Besides, it is as unlikely that workmen would have said nothing about it or that what they said would not have been written into the history of their time as it is that the one-man creator of such a marvel would have kept it so closely secret that no word of it survived him.

No, the lore may be an ass sometimes, but in this case its conviction that the Margate Grotto was originally some kind of shrine and that it was made by Phoenician traders from the Continental mainland anything up to 2,500 years ago is not only more attractive but, on balance, rather more probable, too.

A lot of towns and villages in Kent, no less than anywhere else, can claim that the very origins of their names are part of the county lore. No one, after all, can be certain how some of them acquired the names they bear today, but very few admit that without offering some loreful explanation.

A very good example of that is Headcorn, the Wealden village between Maidstone and Ashford, for which it is claimed that the name began as Hedecron, indicating 'the place of Hydeca's fallen trees'.

Legend, and I believe nothing more substantial, claims that, when Queen Elizabeth I visited the village during one of her progresses, the royal wit was prompted by the excellence of the crops growing in the neighbouring fields to make a joke that 'the name should surely be Hedecorn, not Hedecron'.

The anagram was adopted – and to lend some support to the story, certainly by 1610 it had become the accepted spelling of the name of the village. If the story does nothing else, it serves as a warning against ever jumping to conclusions when trying to guess the origins of place-names.

Mention of Headcorn invites reference to the legendary Headcorn oak – legendary in the sense that legend clings to it like mistletoe to an apple tree and not in any sense implying that its existence is in doubt.

The oak is still there: a riven old shell, still able to don its green finery every year as, according to local belief, it has been doing unfailingly since it first sprang from the parental acorn dropped to the floor of that great Andredsweald, the forest that once covered and left part of its name to the Weald of Kent.

There used to be several Headcorn oaks, all claimed to be at least a thousand years old, but some of them were felled in 1970 because Authority judged them to have become dangerous. Perhaps they had, though they may not have been much more dangerous than the local people whose indignation reached rebellious proportions over it. They rate their oaks very highly in Headcorn, even today.

The remaining oak grows close to the churchyard, and it is well known locally that once a certain John Hessel was wrongly accused of stealing sheep and was imprisoned in a room over the church porch to await justice. But he escaped by climbing along a branch of the old oak tree and so lived to prove his innocence – or abscond from the scene of his guilt, I'm not sure which.

That alone might well have been enough to earn the old tree its local veneration. But it is also said of it that King John, (1199–1216) once sat in its shade to watch bull-baiting and that even before that this was one of those Gospel Oaks beneath which travelling monks preached the Christian gospel to pagan or backsliding Saxons before there was a local church with a pulpit from which to remind them of their Christian duties.

As a matter of fact, trees loom fairly large in Kentish lore, as might be expected of a county that is still well wooded and was once almost wholly given over to untamed forest.

Not that there is anything at all primeval about the Mourning Tree in Bearsted churchyard, a little way along the Ashford Road out of Maidstone. That was planted by a vicar who could not countenance a headstone to mark the grave of nineteen-year-old John Dyke, the last man to be publicly hanged (on Christmas Eve 1830) on Penenden Heath. He was accused of firing a rick, although years after his execution another man made a deathbed confession to the crime, and he was buried on the other side of the churchyard so that his presence should not offend the innocent spirit of his scapegoat. The tree, a Canadian cypress, still marks the spot where the hanged man was buried, but the true culprit's grave is now lost, which is, perhaps, as it should be.

The old yew tree in the churchyard at Loose, on the Hastings side of Maidstone, tells a different and far less likely tale owing much more to lore than to history. There is an old belief in this delightful little mid-Kent village that anyone who sticks a pin in the yew and then runs round it twenty-four times at midnight can peer in through the little window behind one of the churchyard memorials and see a vision in which a woman murders her baby.

All that can be said of that story is that my midnights have been too often otherwise occupied for me to have put it to the test, and my days too few to have found anyone else who would admit to having done so either. Perhaps you might like to try it for yourself?

And then there is Sevenoaks, the West Kent town that probably took its name from the distinguishing landmark of seven oaks on the top of the hill on which the town stands. For much longer then it has been called Sevenoaks, though, it was known as Sennoke, and in the reign of Edward III it gave that name to a very distinguished gentleman who began life unpromisingly enough as a foundling, deserted by his mother in the town and adopted and raised there.

When he grew up, he was apprenticed to a grocer in London and became a friend and colleague of the famous Sir Richard (Dick) Whittington, of pantomime fame. In fact, Sir William Sennoke was Lord Mayor of London before Whittington and became a freeman of the City of London in 1394.

Tradition claims that he fought at Agincourt, single-handed, with the Dauphin of France, who rewarded his skill and courage with a bag of crowns and the words: 'Sennoke, be proud the Dolphyne fought with thee.'

Actually, tradition may be misleading us there, because, if it were not, Sir William Sennoke would have been more than forty years old at the time and an alderman of the City of London, too.

Still, it is a nice story and one that does credit, true or not, to the memory of a man who, after his death in 1432, endowed Seven-oaks School, which is still very much a going concern today.

5

Lore of the Sea

Kent has the longest and most varied coastline of any English county, varying from mudflats and marshes, cliffs and dunes, to shingle and sand, beaches and havens. No wonder that a great deal of the county's lore is associated with the sea and the shore.

Over the centuries, the coastline has provided a living for fishermen and pilots, smugglers and wreckers, bargemen and hoymen, boat-builders and boat-breakers. Kent may be the Garden of England, but its people have not only green fingers but salt in their blood as well.

Many stories are told of the infamous Goodwin Sands – that Ancient Shippe Swallower off the South Thanet coast which has enticed thousands of vessels of all sizes and kinds into its embrace, from which very few indeed have ever escaped. The origins of the Goodwins are themselves the subject of a small volume of lore. The most common belief is that the sandbank was once the Isle of Lomea, just off the Kentish mainland as Thanet once was and Sheppey still is.

Whatever the truth about their origin, even today the Goodwin Sands lie under no more than about twelve feet of water at high tide. At low tide they bask in the sun, firm enough to be visited by novelty-seekers who go there to play football or cricket or, as some London gentlemen did in 1887, to stage a bicycle race.

There have been treasure-hunts, too, and foot- and horse-races, go-karting, picnics and fireworks parties. The brother-in-law of the seventeenth-century diarist John Evelyn was even buried in the Sands in a lead coffin in 1705. So, for that matter, was a certain Francis Merrydith in 1761, although his coffin was subsequently hooked up by a French ship and reburied in Hamburg.

But whatever human frolics the Sands permit at low tide, as soon as the water begins to rise again, the surface becomes unstable and, in parts, turns to deep quicksands capable of sucking down whole ships. In other parts, ships that go aground on the Sands break up as exceptionally strong currents around the sandbank scour away the sand unevenly from beneath the vessel, taking away its support so that it breaks like a dry twig under its own weight and that of the water that breaks over it.

Formerly, vessels wrecked on the Sands in storms often broke up so quickly that they were completely unidentifiable before anyone even knew they were aground. Nowadays, of course, radio, flares and other ship-to-shore emergency communications make that far less common. But it is as true today as ever it was that very few ships wrecked on the Goodwins are refloated. One that was, was the sixteen-thousand-ton Liberian tanker *Panther* in 1971, ending fears of a *Torrey Canyon* type disaster that would have spilled nineteen thousand tons of oil into the Channel and, probably, onto Kent beaches.

Many of the vessels that have been wrecked there over the centuries have carried valuable cargoes, and, despite several serious attempts at treasure-hunts, the Sands remain a tantalizingly inaccessible El Dorado which has so far defied technological advances. One of the great galleons that formed part of the Spanish Armada, after being set on fire by Drake's fireships, drifted onto the Goodwin Sands where it burned to the waterline and disappeared. There has been speculation ever since about whether or not it was one of the war-fleet's treasure ships. If it was, the treasure went to the Goodwins with it and may very well be there still.

More recently, valuable antiques joined the Sands' treasure in August 1964 when the former Brixham trawler *Alessie* sank there. The crew of five were rescued, and so were two cases of valuable antiques. But the rest of the cargo, also of antiques, went down with the ship.

Inevitably, the sea around the Goodwins is well known to seamen to be haunted by the ghosts of past victims. That blazing Armada galleon is said to sail into a spectral re-enactment of its doom. Lightship crews have reported seeing a ship steaming onto the Sands, but always, when their reports were investigated, the ship had vanished, leaving no signs of a recent wreck and no reports of unaccounted-for Channel traffic. It is said that what the lightshipmen really saw was a ghostly Dover-Ostend paddle-steamer, the *Violet*, which went aground on the Goodwin Sands in a snowstorm in 1857 with the loss of everyone aboard.

One of the worst tragedies ever recorded against the dreaded

Sands was in November 1703, when a great storm scattered a fleet of naval ships commanded by Sir Cloudesley Shovel which was anchored in the Downs. Some of the ships fled to safety in the open sea, but sixteen men-o'-war, including four battleships, as well as forty merchantmen, were driven that night onto the Sands with the loss of more than fifteen hundred officers and men. Thanks to the exceptional skill and bravery of Deal lifeboatmen, more than two hundred were saved, although some of those died after they were brought ashore.

The whole episode is very much a part of Kent's coastal lore now, but especially of the stuff of lore is the story of one of those ships, the *Mary*, lost on the Sands with 272 men including Rear-Admiral Beaumont. Only one of the men aboard survived. He was Thomas Atkins, and the story he told was of how he was washed off *Mary* as she broke up, and was flung by the fury of the waves onto the deck of the *Stirling Castle*, a dismasted merchant vessel which was herself already doomed and, in fact, went aground minutes later, shipwrecking the unhappy Atkins for the second time that night. This time he was hurled overboard, directly into the only one of the ship's boats still intact and in which he eventually reached the shore.

A quite different tale, but one equally eligible for inclusion in the lore books, originated in 1747 when a French privateer sighted an English ship, *Fanny*, in the Channel. The Frenchman gave chase, and for eleven hours the *Fanny* evaded her pursuer. At last, her skipper, Captain Blakeley, took his ship clean over the Goodwins, and when the Frenchman tried to follow, it stuck fast and began to sink almost at once.

The tables turned now, Captain Blakeley obeyed the ages-old code of the sea and returned to rescue survivors. He lived to bless – or possibly to rue – the day (these old stories are often diplomatically vague about such important matters), for among the survivors was his own wife, who had been a passenger on a ship that had been taken by the same French privateer some time earlier.

Then there was the story of the barque *Reliance*, wrecked on the Goodwins in January 1857. She broke up, and among her salvaged cargo was a chest full of soap. As a routine precaution, Customs men probed the soap with steel rods and were as surprised as anyone when their diligence disclosed, inside a smaller box hidden in the soap, a decomposing human head which had been hacked off some time before. Apart from the fact that the head seemed once to have belonged to a Malay or Philippino male, it was never identified and joined an enormous number of unsolved mysteries of the sea.

In both World Wars the Goodwin Sands loyally claimed their share of enemy shipping. In November 1917 the U-boat *U-48* ran aground on the north-west end of the Sands and went down trying to fight off a pursuing destroyer. The submarine is still there, and from time to time the shifting sands reveal the mouldering hulk, like a trophy of which the great Shippe Swallower is particularly proud.

In November 1919 the Estonian schooner *Toogo* was lost during the night on the Goodwins, and although Deal lifeboatmen got near enough to the wreck to see the crew and the skipper's wife clinging to the ship's rigging, before they were able to close in for the rescue, a huge wave dashed over the stranded vessel, and she disappeared, taking everyone on board with her. Ever since, lightshipmen have added the ghostly cries of the only woman aboard the *Toogo* to their list of Goodwins hauntings.

One of the saddest little stories of the Goodwins wrecks, though, is perhaps that of the *Lady Lovibund*, which is also said to haunt the sandbank periodically, some say every fiftieth anniversary of her tragic end. The *Lady Lovibund* left London on 13 February 1748, skippered by Captain Simon Reed and the beautiful young wife he had married only hours before sailing, Annetta.

At the helm was Captain Reed's best friend, the *Lady Lovibund*'s mate. He, too, had loved Annetta and, having lost her to his captain, he spitefully steered the ship on a course that grounded her on the Goodwins. Although the weather was calm at the time, and the Deal boatmen put out to go to the rescue, the *Lady Lovibund* sank before their eyes. By the time the Deal men reached the spot, she had vanished, leaving no trace. The vengeful mate presumably went down with her as well as the captain and his lovely young bride, which put him out of reach of the law but entangled him in the Goodwins lore for ever.

Smuggling has been a major business all round the Kent coast ever since the idea of taxing the import and export of goods was first put into practice. Over the centuries, many tales of smugglers and their exploits have threaded their way into the tapestry of Kent lore.

Like the incident in nineteenth-century Folkestone, where a Mr and Mrs Robinson were in bed in their home on the Warren one dark night when servants were aroused by an insistent knocking on the door. When the door was opened, a small band of men forced their way inside and, pushing the servants out of their way, went upstairs to the bedroom where the Robinsons were still in bed.

The strangers woke them up and peremptorily ordered them to get out of the bed. When the couple stood shivering, as much with fright as with cold, no doubt, on the far side of the big bed, the intruders lifted up the feather mattress and stowed away several mysterious and apparently heavy packages underneath it. That done, they put the mattress back and warned the Robinsons: 'Silence – or death!' Then they left the shocked couple to return to their bed.

Hours later, as Mr and Mrs Robinson were just getting their shattered nerves under control enough to begin to hope they might get some sleep that night after all, they were visited by Excisemen who demanded to be allowed to search the house. Once again, the couple dragged themselves from the bed and watched in the utmost trepidation while the search was carried out. Luckily, the officials found nothing, and the luckless householders were left to recover from the second invasion of their privacy in one night.

But it was just not the Robinsons' night. Just before dawn, back came the first band, again bursting into the house and tipping the hapless couple unceremoniously out of their bed yet again. When they had reclaimed their hidden packages from under the mattress, it was found that the extra weight had broken the bed.

The strangers promised that Mr Robinson should be rewarded for his 'co-operation', and the bed mended for him as well. But Mr Robinson decided that enough was enough. He declined the offered reward and had the bed repaired at his own expense – and probably felt he was quite well enough rewarded if nothing like that night's experience ever befell him and his wife again.

The bed stands today in one of the rooms of Lympne Castle, where a notice tells the tale for the hundreds of visitors who see it every year.

Smuggling was comparatively safe and easy until the seventeenth century, when Customs and Excise began to be better organized to try to stop the steady drain on national income. Many people condemned the laws rather than the smugglers, seeing them as attacks on their ages-old right of free trading. Smugglers were widely supported, and they were able to carry on their work almost openly, confident of the protection of leaders of the community.

As the struggle to enforce the law became more bitter, smuggling became more dangerous. Runs worth tens of thousands of pounds were landed and taken inland to the hides and storehouses from which they were distributed to customers. The men who masterminded these valuable runs could not afford to lose such big consignments if they were waylaid by the law-enforcement officers, so they recruited their own private armies of ruffians prepared to guard the illicit cargoes with their lives – or, preferably, by taking the lives of the officers the authorities sent against them – if need be.

Throughout the eighteenth and nineteenth centuries, the history of smuggling in Kent is scarred with a number of pitched battles, many of which were won quite decisively by the outlaws. Among the gangs, probably the most famous, or infamous, was the eighteenth-century Hawkhurst Gang, led by the three Kingsmell brothers, Thomas, Richard and George, of Goudhurst. They fought several battles with riding officers and dragoons, but the most memorable of all their engagements was the one they lost in April 1747 to a scratch force of volunteer village militiamen.

The clash might never have happened if the gangsters had stuck to smuggling. But when there was no smuggling, because of the weather, for instance, they turned equally readily to highway robbery and outright banditry, raiding farms and villages and helping themselves to whatever they wanted. They regarded most of the Weald as 'their' territory, and they imposed a reign of terror with the most vicious summary 'justice' for anyone so much as suspected of betraying them or crossing them in any way.

At last the villagers of Goudhurst banded together, and, led by an ex-corporal recently discharged from the Army, a man called William Sturt who later became Goudhurst's Poor House Master, they formed their own Goudhurst Militia to defend their homes against the gangsters.

The Kingsmells heard about the militia and sent a contemptuous message to Sturt, telling him they would ride into Goudhurst and teach the villagers a lesson they would not forget.

But when they came, the villagers were ready for them. There was a pitched battle around the church and the nearby inn, in which two of the Kingsmell brothers were killed before the rest of the gang turned and fled.

That was the beginning of the end of the Hawkhurst Gang, but the Battle of Goudhurst, as it came to be known, added another colourful episode to Kentish lore. It was not, of course, an end of smuggling. Almost a century later, in 1821, there was another major battle between smugglers and law-enforcement officers which is remembered today as the Battle of Brookland. That one featured the Aldington Gang, which was every bit as notorious as, and perhaps even more unscrupulously vicious than, the Hawkhurst Gang had been a century earlier.

Indeed, smuggling has never entirely died out, and from time to time headlines in the national Press reveal that old habits are dying hard in the Kentish ports. Today, the cargoes are most often drugs or pornographic books and films, and the technology employed by both sides is much more sophisticated. But the effects of smuggling remain the same – huge profits for the smugglers and massive losses of revenue for the national exchequer.

Until the middle of the present century, Kent's coast and waterways were busy with sailing vessels of all kinds. The barges, with their characteristic ochred sails, were the workhorses of the waterways, supremely practical yet with a certain gracefulness that is appreciated more today than it was at the time, probably.

Inevitably, the barges and the people who worked them collected a substantial body of lore all to themselves and, as seems to be the way of all watermen, fresh or salt, everywhere their yarns have a touch of incredibility sometimes lacking in more landlocked lore.

Whole books have been written about the barges, many of them relying heavily upon the recollections of old bargemen and therefore wholly legitimately lore. Many of the old captains and members of their crews were colourful characters themselves, but it was the barges that stole the limelight.

Zebrina, for example, was a Whitstable built barge of some 185 tons, registered at Faversham in 1873. After working both English and South American coastal waters, she left Falmouth in October 1917 with a cargo of Swansea coal, bound for St Brieuc, in France.

Two days later, she was found ashore on Rozel Point, south of Cherbourg.

Her hull was undamaged, her rigging only slightly disordered – not enough to explain why she was beached. But most mysterious of all, there was not a soul aboard, and nor was anything ever heard of the crew again. Thus *Zebrina* joined that select fleet of vessels, of which the *Marie Celeste* is surely the flagship, that have down the years contributed some of the most intriguing incidents to the unfailingly fascinating lore of the sea.

Then there was *Ena*. She was one of sixteen barges that were sent to France in 1940 to help with the Dunkirk evacuation. Like others in that flotilla of little ships, the barges carried supplies and ammunition out to the desperate rearguard defenders and returned with men plucked from the beleaguered beaches. But *Ena* distinguished herself by fulfilling the old sailor-man's contention that ships have personalities of their own and tolerate rather than really need human crews.

For the barge was abandoned, anchored in Dunkirk Roads, and written off as lost by her owners. But lost she certainly was not, for some time later she turned up on Sandwich Flats, on Kent's south coast, empty and slightly damaged but still seaworthy, having apparently weighed her own anchor and found her own way home.

Even older than smuggling and the barge trade, wrecking was a respectable Kent coast occupation for centuries. It was not, in fact, always a nefarious business, with heartless self-seekers luring ships onto rocks with callous disregard for life. Wrecking did not mean causing a wreck so much as benefiting from it. It was allied to beachcombing, with no laws to forbid coast-dwellers to help themselves to whatever was washed ashore from wrecks at sea. Indeed, it was legitimate enough for boatmen to go out to a wreck and help themselves to whatever they could salvage – which often resulted in a near-intact vessel being literally taken to pieces, and timbers, ropework, metalwork and anything else that could be cut, prised or torn away carried off.

Bureaucracy later qualified the legitimacy of this perquisite of life beside the sea by defining a wreck as such only if there was no living creature – including the ship's pet – left alive aboard. Inevitably, that meant that it was not unknown for the abject poverty of fishermen prevented by weather from pursuing their livelihood to stand back and watch a ship being pounded to death and everyone aboard being swept away rather than attempting a rescue. Only when the piteous cries were finally silenced would they launch their own boats and start the work of salvaging all they could either for their own use or to be sold.

More recently, of course, the wreckers' descendants have become the heroes of the lifeboat and have turned their very considerable skills of seamanship, once employed in competition with each other for the prime loot from the wrecks, to saving thousands of lives that would certainly have been lost in the days of the wreckers.

Dover and Deal – and especially Deal – wrote their own chapter in the county's lore with their beach-launched luggers in which the townsmen made a speciality of ferrying supplies out to the ships anchored in the Downs, like seaborne travelling salesmen.

Prior to the second half of the eighteenth century, coastal towns and villages were generally regarded by people living further inland as invariably poor, unhealthy and to be avoided if at all possible. Usually it was not only possible but easy, of course, and so the portsmen were left very much to themselves, to get on with the particularly arduous, hazardous and economically precarious lives they led, as best they could.

But then, slowly, it began to be fashionable to 'slum it' beside the sea. Some of the very best people began to build themselves holiday homes near the sea, and the practice really took off after 'Prinny' (the Prince of Wales, who became King George IV in 1820) made himself patron of Brighton and turned it into a sort of London by the sea where no one who was anyone could afford not to be seen during the season.

Not long after that, the railways opened up more of the coast to more of the people. Soon, cheap day trips were pouring Londoners into Kent resorts like Ramsgate and Broadstairs, and after that came the building boom as the trippers returned to live where once they had paddled their feet.

Today, parts of the south coast are characterized by miles of chalets and caravans and more permanent homes, too, and the heyday of the seaside home dream is probably already past. No doubt, one day, it too will be remembered mainly for the fragments of lore that cling to its remains, just as today old buildings and topographical features recall loreful tales of the smugglers and the wreckers, luggermen and bargemen, fishermen and lifeboatmen of former times.

6

Sacred and Profane Lore

The stories of the lives and miracles of resident Kentish saints are many, most of them rooted in the county's very early history.

Although we know that Christian worship was not unknown in this corner of the country during Roman times, it left very few traces that survived the troubled times that followed. The first waves of Jutish settlers were, certainly for the most part, at least, pagan. They were not unaware of Christianity, but it was an alien religion that had never had much impact upon their own culture.

When Augustine arrived from Rome with his party of forty monks in 597, he came to a Kent where there were a few Christians – the Queen, Bertha, was one – but where most, including King Ethelbert, were pagan. It was the Queen who persuaded her husband to allow the monks to land at Ebbsfleet in the Isle of Thanet, and no doubt it was she who persuaded him to go to meet them, too.

It is said that at first Ethelbert was reluctant to have anything at all to do with the missionaries, but when he finally agreed to meet them, he stipulated that it must be in the open, apparently judging that any Christian magic would be less effective where his own gods, who tended to be a pretty robust outdoor-type lot, could keep an eye on the proceedings.

As a result of the meeting – or possibly even more as a result of some determined domestic lobbying by Bertha – Ethelbert finally allowed Augustine to use the even then ancient church of St Martin outside the Canterbury city wall, and in the end went so far as to succumb to baptism, possibly in the font in St Martin's, and so begin a mass conversion that made the whole of Kent at least nominally Christian within a few short years of the monks' arrival.

Common lore claims that Ethelbert was baptized in the Swale, that arm of the Thames and Medway estuary that separates the Isle of Sheppey from the mainland, on Whit Sunday 597, and that

70

on Christmas Day that same year then thousand of his subjects followed the royal example.

Augustine stayed in the city to build both the abbey that later took his name (and is today no more than represented by a few excavated ruins) and the monastery, the Christ Church of which became Canterbury Cathedral.

Augustine was credited with a number of miracles during his lifetime. On one occasion, when the Christians at Canterbury were being blamed by pagans in the nearby Elham valley for the disastrous drought that was threatening their crops, Augustine went to see them. They were less than welcoming, but he knelt down among them and prayed for a miracle that would demonstrate that their suspicions about the Christians were unfounded and also relieve their anxieties about their crops.

According to legend, where he knelt a spring of clear water gushed forth to irrigate the parched land. Such a demonstration might well have been enough to have converted the pagans on the spot, but their own gods, recognizing the challenge, caused a great storm to tear up trees and block the new stream before it could properly begin its relief-bringing mission in life. Luckily for Augustine, though, his God had already had a great deal of practice in having the last word in situations of this kind. He chose not to undo what the Norse gods had done, but instead decreed that henceforth the stream should flow freely once every seven years as a regular reminder of His presence and power.

One of the earliest religious communities in Kent was that founded by Queen Ermenburga of Northumbria in Thanet. She was given the land after her cousin, King Egbert of Kent, accepted responsibility for the murder of her two young brothers. Ermenburga built her monastery in about 675 in what is now the parish of Minster in Thanet, took the religious name of Domneva and was pretty well ignored by both history and legend from that time on.

But she did have a daughter, Mildred, who succeeded her as abbess, and she was canonized and became the patron saint of Thanet, about whom several stories are remembered. Once, when she returned to England after she had been living in France for some time, she is said to have left the imprint of her foot permanently on the first stone she trod upon. The same story claims that, although the stone was removed several times, it always returned, of its own accord, to the same place.

Probably the best-known of all St Mildred's miraculous feats was her emergence from a hot oven after three hours, completely unharmed by the experience. On another occasion, her holiness was tested by the Devil himself, who found her in her chamber at prayer by candlelight. Mischievously, he blew out the candle, but instantly it was relit by the Abbess's guardian angel, whereupon Old Nick admitted defeat and bothered the Holy Mother no more.

Few of the early Christian saints were commoners, and many of them were members of royal families. Like Edith, daughter of Edgar, who was crowned first King of All England in May 973. Edith was reputedly born at Kemsing, near Sevenoaks, where it is still possible to visit St Edith's Well, once in the gardens of a convent, the waters of which were said to have been endowed with healing powers by the holiness of her presence there.

Saintly brothers who left their mark on Faversham were Crispin and Crispianus. They were Romans who left the city during the Christian persecutions of Diocletian and Maximin in the third century. They travelled to Britain and settled in the little creekside town and port of Faversham where they set up shop as shoemakers. Tradition tells how they preached by day and worked by night, making shoes which they sold cheaply to the poor from leather that was delivered to them by an angel.

One version of their story tells how they were thrown into the creek by Roman soldiers but were saved from drowning by divine intervention. But they were martyred finally, probably by being beheaded at Soissons in France in about 287. Some say their relics were returned to Faversham, where they were later thrown into the sea and were washed ashore at Romney Marsh.

Certainly, the brothers became the patron saints of shoemakers, and, centuries later, there was an altar dedicated to them in Faversham church. Their day, 25 October, on which the Battle of Agincourt was fought in 1415, was celebrated specially in Faversham at least until the Reformation.

Probably the most celebrated of all the Kentish saints was the twelfth-century archbishop Thomas Becket. Becket was not a native of Kent, having been born in London in 1118, son of Gilbert, a Norman knight and merchant. Thomas's friendship with King Henry II, their quarrel and his murder in December 1170 by four knights who believed they were serving their King's unspoken wish, is familiar history throughout Christendom.

Becket began to make his impact upon the lore within three days of his burial, when his first miracle was claimed for him by a woman who appealed to him as a saint, on behalf of her sick son. By Easter 1171 Canterbury was already a place of pilgrimage to the shrine of the new saint, who has not, nevertheless, canonized until 1173.

It was probably not until after his death that stories began to circulate about some of the more saintly aspects of his life. For instance, Lambarde recorded a story that, when Becket was walking in the Old Park of the Archbishop's palace at Otford one day, busy with his prayers, he found it difficult to concentrate because of the persistent song of a nightingale in a nearby bush. He commanded the bird to desist and added also that thenceforth no bird of that kind should ever be so bold as to sing in the Park again – although later writers noted that either the ban was lifted or it lost its potency after a while, for nightingales have been heard there in comparatively recent times.

The palace at Otford, in fact, was said to owe its water supply to St Thomas' Well, which burst forth from the ground where Becket struck his staff one day.

Archbishop Becket is also lorefully credited with responsibility for a nickname that clung to Kentish Men for a long time after the martyrdom. It seems that there was a certain rivalry between Rochester and Canterbury which led, on one occasion when Becket visited the Medway Towns, to his being treated with a good deal less respect and courtesy than he felt his office entitled him to. Some ruffians in Strood, in fact, were not content with limiting their barracking to verbal jibes. One of them took shears to the back of the horse on which the primate was travelling and docked its tail.

Becket, who was all man for all his archiepiscopal saintliness, and had a quick temper, responded by cursing not merely the perpetrator of the insult but all his fellows and all their sons, too, for ever, so that they were condemned from that day on to be known as 'Kentish longtails' from the retributory tail that grew on every Kentish Man.

In point of fact, a very similar story is told of St Augustine, who felt called upon to teach the pagan Kentish Men a sharp lesson when they mocked him during one of his preaching tours of the kingdom.

Whichever prospective saint it was who actually bestowed the tail and the derisory nickname upon the Kentish longtails, I think it only right at this point to record that, despite having been born a Kentish Man myself, I can discern no tail on me. Perhaps the mortal curse was lifted by the forgiving sanctity of canonization.

In about 1165, there was born in Kent, of noble parents, a man called Simon who, at the age of twelve, left home to live the life of a hermit in the hollow trunk of a tree. Tradition sites the tree at Stockbury, today a pleasant little village on the north slopes of the North Downs overlooking the Swale and the Isle of Sheppey, and named after the hermit had renounced his family name in favour of the name Stock (or tree trunk), to which, by then, he no doubt felt rather closer.

After twenty years of living thus, he joined the Carmelite Order, either when they came to England in 1241 or while on a visit to the Holy Land on pilgrimage. Either way, history relates that he was elected General of the Order at Aylesford Chapter in 1247 and specially modified the Order, travelling widely to do so. He died in Bordeaux in 1265, and his body was brought back to Aylesford, where he is still remembered as the Order's first Prior General.

One of the most unlikely Kent saints was a humble baker when he set out from Perth. He was a good man, who apparently made a practice of giving every tenth loaf he baked to the poor.

In 1201 he set out to go on a pilgrimage to the Holy Land, travelling via Canterbury, and had reached Rochester when his servant robbed and murdered him. The monks at Rochester took charge of the body and gave him a suitable burial in their choir. They had long felt comparatively neglected in the pilgrimage stakes, especially since St Thomas Becket had become so popular and was drawing vast crowds of pilgrims to Canterbury, very much to the benefit of the city and the monks who lived there.

So Rochester put in a claim for their own William of Perth to be canonized, and, finally, he was, becoming St William in 1256. His shrine at Rochester never really rivalled that of St Thomas at Canterbury, but at least the Kentish Men felt at last that they could hold up their heads in the company of the Men of Kent when it came to the question of saints.

Before we leave Canterbury and its unique place in Christian lore, we ought to note that more than once the safety of the cathedral itself has been credited to miraculous intervention. Such was certainly the claim when, in the seventh century,

Archbishop Mellitus prayed for a change of wind to save Canterbury Cathedral from being burned to the ground in a disastrous city fire. The wind did change, and the cathedral was saved.

A rather more corporate effort was needed in 1942 when Canterbury was blitzed with firebombs that rained down all round the cathedral, ringing it with burning buildings yet leaving it standing at the end of the ordeal virtually unscarred. Firemen and volunteer firewatchers probably prayed no less fervently than Mellitus, and certainly there were believers a-plenty when the raids ended to claim that the cathedral's escape was no less miraculous in the twentieth century than it had been in the seventh.

I suppose most churches have their own individual tales to tell about their pasts. The East Kent colliery village of Chislet, for instance, remembers that it once had a priest who was never seen by his parishioners, from whom he received food in return for a blessing given from a small window they could not see into.

On the North Kent marshes, the church of St Mary's, Hoo, recalls that it once had as its rector that Reverend Robert Burt who bought the living with hush-money paid to him in 1785 for marrying secretly and illegally Maria Fitzherbert and the Prince of Wales, later to be King George IV. The secret did not come to light for 114 years after the ceremony, and during that time the Reverend Robert Gascoyne Burt, son of the conspirator, had added his own eccentricity to the local lore by making it a rule never to allow men, women and children to mingle in his church and never to preach a sermon in all the fifty-nine years he conducted services there.

Eastwards along the North Kent coast, Reculver is instantly recognizable by the twin towers that are all that remain of the former Saxon church there. After the church fell into disrepair and was dismantled by parishioners who found other uses for stone, wood and lead, the towers were bought and maintained by Trinity House as a landmark for shipping.

It also had the virtue of keeping alive the legend that the towers were modelled upon those of Davington Priory, just outside Faversham, at the wishes of a twelfth-century prioress who, while travelling by sea to Broadstairs with her sister, was shipwrecked in a storm off Reculver. The prioress was saved, but her sister was drowned, and the legend claims that, as a thanksgiving for her own deliverance as well as a memorial to her sister, she had the towers built so that they would be a prominent landmark to warn seamen of the dangers of the coast at this point.

Down on Romney Marsh there is a tiny church at Fairfield which is distinguished with the reputation of being one of the oldest Kent churches still in use, and which has the unusual feature of a grassy causeway built out to it from the main road so that worshippers and visitors can reach it when the surrounding marshland is flooded, something that happened rather more often in the past than it does today.

It is also unusual in that it is dedicated to St Thomas Becket, and the reason for that, so 'they' say, is that once an archbishop of Canterbury was journeying across Romney Marsh when he fell into one of the many dykes and ditches that criss-cross the region. Romney Marsh is a pretty desolate-looking place, in parts, even today; then it must have seemed like a desert indeed to the floundering primate, and he prayed to St Thomas as he came up for the second time for the miracle that alone could save him from an otherwise inevitable watery death.

In the nick of time, along came a local farmer, who saw him and hauled him back to the land of the living, in gratitude for which (though whether the farmer saw it in that light, we do not know) the Archbishop had the little church built and personally dedicated it to St Thomas Becket.

Not far from Fairfield, still on the Marsh, is the St Augustine's Church at Brookland that always gets its pictures in the guidebooks because of its unique (in Kent) candle-snuffer detached bell-tower. The tower was built in about 1450, probably for the prosaic but fairly uncolourful reason that the foundations of the church itself were not firm enough to support its extra weight. But that reason is not, of course, good enough for the local lore-makers, who have dreamed up several reasons for its being where it is.

The one I like best is that which tells how the parish of Brookland went through a period of moral laxity during which nobody came to church to be married any more. But then, one day, along came a young couple to the church to ask the vicar to marry them. Their request was so extraordinary that the church shuddered to hear it, and the bell-tower jumped down and settled itself where it is now to be seen today.

Back in central Kent, near Maidstone, one of the great church treasures of the county is the magnificent Culpepper altar-cloth of

All Saints Church at Hollingbourne. The cloth was embroidered three hundred years ago: ten feet of purple velvet worked in gold thread with representations of all sorts of fruits. It was the work of the daughters of Sir Thomas Culpepper – Colpeper, Culpeper, Colepepper: spell it any way you like, they did! – who was a Royalist during the Civil War and who shared the exile of Charles II for twelve years.

During that period, according to local lore, his daughters busied themselves, while they waited loyally for their father's return, with embroidering the altar-cloth, working sometimes by such poor light that one of them actually went blind before the job was done.

Incidentally, while we are with the Culpepper family, although not exactly lore in that the evidence for it is very (if not literally) concrete, the superb white marble figure of the girls' mother, Elizabeth, is still to be marvelled at inside the church. At her feet is a fabulous creature with a dog's head, leopard's spots, lion's tail and cloven hooves – no wonder it is represented chained to the spot. But the inscription has given the Lady Elizabeth a place in county lore, for, with whatever degree of sincerity or accuracy, it describes her as 'The best woman, the best wife, and the best mother', which makes her a paragon such as delights the lore.

One more example? Well, not very far from Hollingbourne is the village of Bearsted, almost an extension of the county town of Maidstone now but once very definitely distinct and separate.

Bearsted has, however, kept its village green, on one side of which is the church. The tower of the church is embellished with three mysterious stone beasts, one on each of three corners. No one has ever been able to say with any sort of finality what the creatures are supposed to be, or why they were put there. Indeed, pretty well all that is known about them, locally at any rate, is that on one night of every year the three jump down from the top of the tower, stretch their legs a bit on the green and then – always without being seen – return to their perches to gaze over the surrounding roofscape with stony stoicism for another 365 days.

So much, then, for sacred lore in Kent. If God's work has left its mark on the county, so has the Devil's, too. Several legends tell of Satanic visitations, and the Devil's disciples have made their presence felt more than once.

At the entrance to Newington churchyard, near Sittingbourne, is the Devil's Stone. It is, in fact, one of two sarsen stones and not, in itself, specially demonic at all. But the story is told that on one occasion the Devil was so enraged by the ringing of Newington church bells that one night he climbed the tower of the church and stole the bells, taking them away with him in a sack.

In jumping down from the tower, however, he landed on one of the stones and fell over. The bells spilled out from the sack and rolled down the lane to Halstow, where they were lost in a stream which – naturally enough – has run as clear as a bell ever since!

Perhaps it was the same visitation, for it was not very far from Newington, when the Devil left marks on the tower of Rainham church when he tried to push the tower over. He failed, of course, but not until he had blunted his fingernails on the stonework with the fury of his attack and left the marks there.

The Countless Stones at the bottom of Blue Bell Hill, between Maidstone and Chatham, have already been referred to (see 'Lore of the Land') for the legend that their number is a secret kept by the Devil himself.

Several places in Kent bear the Devil's name, not always for obvious reasons. Indeed, in most cases the reason, if ever there was one, has been lost, even in lore.

Close to the Surrey border, near where the River Medway is joined by the Eden brook, there is a medieval earthwork known as Devil's Den, and there is another Devil's Den near Hollingbourne village. The Devil's Kneading-trough is a physical feature of Crundale Downs near Wye: a steep-sided natural bowl and part of a very lovely part of the protected countryside of Kent – not at all the sort of place that seems to deserve such a dread association.

A remote corner of the Somerhill estate at Tonbridge is known as Devil's Gill, once the site of one of the many medieval iron bloomeries that flourished throughout the Weald of Kent when wood and the charcoal derived from it made this the industrial centre of England before coal-mining changed all that.

Near the Three Went Ways, between Pluckley and Smarden in East Kent, there is a Devil's Bush, from which local pranksters will tell you the Devil himself can be persuaded to leap out at you – if that is what you want – if you will just run round the bush three times backwards. There is, I might say, a good deal of difference of local opinion about just which is the right bush, although there seems to be a general recognition that it is one of them.

At Farningham, in the churchyard behind the church, local girls used to claim that, by throwing a pin through a hole in the tomb of the square-domed mausoleum of Thomas Nash (uncle of John Nash, architect of Brighton Royal Pavilion and other lesser extravagances), they could induce the Devil to peer out of the hole at them. If you have ever tried to throw a pin through a hole in anything at all, you will be easily persuaded that there were very few eye-witnesses to the truth of this rather curious conviction.

Kent was never a particular hotbed of witchcraft, although it was not without its witches, or at any rate the poor wretches who were accused of practising witchcraft.

Reynold Scott, one of the more enlightened sixteenth-century sceptics about the subject, recorded how in 1581 a certain Margaret Simons was arraigned for witchcraft at Rochester Assizes, accused by Brenchley vicar John Ferrall of bewitching his son.

The son (who was known locally, apparently, as 'an ungratious boie') evidently passed by Margaret's home one day and her dog barked at him, whereupon the boy drew a knife and chased the dog to the house door. He was seen threatening the dog by its owner, who came to the door, rebuked the boy and shooed him away.

Within a week of the incident, the boy fell sick. In his bed, with nothing better to occupy his mind, he recalled having chased Margaret Simons' dog and told his father how the woman had told him off for it. His father, deeming this to be clear evidence that the lad had been bewitched, called in another local witch, who cured his son. The cure settled it as far as the vicar was concerned, and he laid information against Margaret, and she was duly brought to trial. She might very well have hung as a witch, too, but one juror refused to condemn her, and she was saved from the gallows.

During the mid-seventeenth-century witch hunts, there were a number of notable witchcraft trials in Kent. Scott, in his book *Discovery of Witchcraft*, also told how, on 27 January 1572, ten devils were driven out of a twenty-three-year-old Dutchman by one John Sticklebow. The claim was supported by the mayor and prominent townsfolk in Maidstone, where it happened, but the whole thing was later dismissed as a fraud, which could not have done the mayor and his prominent townsfolk much good in the community.

In 1574 a seventeen-year-old girl, Mildred Norrington, was a servant in the home of William Spooner of Westwell, near Ashford, when she became possessed of the Devil. At least, that was the judgement of a crowd of experts who gathered and prayed for the casting-out of the Devil, which roared his defiance through the girl's mouth and made her so violent that it took four strong men to hold her down.

In the end, though, the Devil admitted in so many words that, although he had taken up residence in the girl, he had been unable to harm her because, he said, 'God kept her.' During this rather remarkable confession, however, the Devil named an old woman called Alice, who, he said, had shut him up in two bottles and sent him to Mildred.

Well, obviously the witnesses to this account of what had happened could not take the word of the Devil, a notoriously unreliable custodian of the truth, so they made a search of the house for some evidence. Sure enough, they found one of the very bottles behind the wall at the back of old Alice's house. The Devil further confessed that he was kept by his mistress, Alice, to kill people she did not like, or who did not like her, and he named three people he had already killed for her.

Just what was the ultimate fate of old Alice is not clear, but it seems that the prayers of the experts gathered around poor possessed Mildred finally triumphed and the Devil was compelled to leave her.

In the 1580s, in Town Malling, an archer was brought to trial for witchcraft because he was a particularly good shot with his bow. The local people persuaded themselves that he had a familiar demon, which took the form of a fly and which helped him win bets with his arrows. The man was found guilty and punished, and we can assume that the standard of archery in Town Malling fell off noticeably after that.

In 1648 Dorothy Avery and Thomas Creed of Cranbrook were were tried and acquitted of a charge of being witches, but four other Cranbrook women were found guilty and executed at Maidstone.

At Faversham, the mayor and magistrates were given special powers during the Civil War when committals by local magistrates to assizes were interrupted and all justice was dispensed locally by special commissions, empowered to sit as assize judges. Among the cases brought to the Faversham commissioners was one in which four old ladies were accused of witchcraft. The mayor at the time – 1645 – was Robert Greenstreet, and he seems to have been particularly ill disposed towards witches. The accused were Joan Walliford (or Willford), Joan Cariden, Jane Hott and Elizabeth Harris, all accused by Thomas Gardler, who declared he was bewitched by the widow Walliford after he fell out of a window.

Questioned, the widow confessed that she had been visited by the Devil in the form of a little dog some seven years before, and that she had made a pact which she signed in her own blood. The Devil, she said, had then sent her a familiar called Bunn, and it was he who caused Thomas Gardler to fall from the window and hurt himself. In condemning herself, Joan named her three friends as associates in witchcraft, going so far as to say that Joan Cariden had even cursed the mayor.

At the trial, Joan Cariden told of a local coven which held a sabbat at which the Devil himself presided. Jane Hott denied all the charges, although she did admit that a thing like a hedgehog, but soft as a cat, had come to her twenty years before and returned regularly ever since.

Elizabeth Harris confessed to murder by witchcraft, but her execution was postponed, and records are not clear that she was, in fact, ever executed at all. The others, however, were all found guilty and hanged within a few days.

In New Romney there lingers a story about a famous witch-finder, Old Mother Baker. On one occasion she was asked by the parents of a sick girl to seek out the witch who was the cause of the girl's illness, and Mother Baker confirmed the family's own suspicions that the cause of the mischief was a neighbour, whose home was accordingly searched by the old witch-finder herself. Sure enough, a waxen heart was found, with needles and other sharp instruments stuck into it. The case, it seemed, was proved.

Luckily for the neighbour, though, she had friends who were not convinced about the witch-finding talents of Mother Baker, and they swore they had seen her take the evidence out of a big bag she carried about with her and plant it where she said she had found it. Whether they really did see any such thing or not may be in as much doubt as Old Mother Baker's witch-finding prowess, but nevertheless she was duly tried for fraud, and her career was ended.

Certainly one of the biggest of the Kent witch trials was at Maidstone in 1652, before the assizes which started there on 30 July. Six women were charged with witchcraft: Anne Ashby, Anne Martyn, Mary Browne, Mildred Wright, Anne Wilson and Mary Reade. The first five were from Cranbrook and the sixth from Lenham. Anne Ashby and Anne Martyn were both self-confessed witches, and during the trial Ashby had some kind of seizure during which she was seen to swell to 'a monstrous and vast bigness'.

A macabre exhibit at the trial was a piece of scorched flesh which Ashby claimed was given to her by the Devil and which any of them had only to touch for their wishes to be granted. The power of the talisman deserted them at the trial, though, for they were all found guilty and condemned to death.

Ashby and Martyn both claimed to be pregnant by the Devil, and reprieves were sought. They were eventually granted, too, although not in time to save the pair, who were both hanged in defiance of a good deal of public pressure for burning.

They were accused of the devilish crime of having bewitched nine children, one man and one woman, and of causing the loss of £500-worth of cattle and much corn at sea.

The Reverend Richard Barham, author of the *Ingoldsby Legends*, had his tongue pretty firmly in his cheek, as he so often had, when he wrote his famous assertion that 'The world, according to the best geographers, is divided into Europe, Asia, Africa, America, and Romney Marsh. In this last named, and fifth, quarter of the globe, a witch may still be discovered in stormy season, careering on her broomstick over Dymchurch Wall.'

But earlier generations had taken the threat of witchcraft very seriously indeed. Mayors of Sandwich, for instance, have for centures carried – and, in fact, still carry – a blackthorn wand of office as a safeguard against witches.

7

War Lore

War always creates its own legends, and Kent's unique proximity to European battlefields has always tended to give it a prominent role in those legends, and to bring some of them onto Kentish soil itself.

The county has been a battlefield many times. Although history has very little to tell us on the subject, and lore has nothing to add, no doubt there were skirmishes and even battles over land occupation in Kent long before Caesar began coming, seeing and conquering. Certainly, his exploratory landing in 55 BC was met with what seems to have been a fairly experienced sort of resistance on the beaches around Deal, and in 54 BC his second expeditionary force of five legions, about 35,000 men, waded ashore in Sandwich Bay and had to win a pitched battle at the Chilham crossing of the River Stour before it could advance any further into the country.

When the third Roman force, this time under the command of Aulus Plautius, came to stay in AD 43, they, too, had to fight their way across the first main obstacle, the River Stour, where their advance was challenged by the forces of two British chiefs, Caractacus and Togodumnus. The Britons were forced back, first to the River Medway and then to the River Thames, where there were more battles, one lasting two whole days, before the invaders could march on London.

The Aulus Plautius Roman invasion soon moved on past Kent, going north. There was no need for big garrisons in Kent. Gaul was Roman and secure behind the Rhine frontier, so all southern England needed was policing and administering. London was already an important trading-post and soon became a major Roman town, and in any case Britons in the south had for many years been casting envious glances towards the higher standards of living and creature comforts that demonstrably came with inclusion in the Roman Empire on the other side of the Channel, and were not particularly unwilling to join, anyway.

They did not welcome the invaders, but once the occupation forces moved on northwards, they did not mind all that much and soon settled down to make the best of things. Within a century, the 'Romans' in Britain were mostly native-born Britons living under Roman law and custom, and that continued for the four hundred years during which Britain was part of the Empire.

When 'the Romans' left, it was no mass exodus but the gradual withdrawal of Roman support – not unlike the British withdrawal from India during this century – leaving the Roman-British unprotected from the increasingly determined raids of Saxon (North European) pirates. It took something like two hundred years for Roman Britain to disintegrate altogether.

Towards the end of the Roman period the Saxons were becoming such a nuisance that a Count of the Saxon Shore was appointed to take charge of a series of eleven great forts built to defend the coast from the Wash to the Isle of Wight. Four of those forts were in Kent, at what are now Reculver, Richborough, Dover and Lympne. Today the remains known as Stutfall Castle mark the site of the Roman Portus Lemanis, on the estuary of the old River Limen.

The Romans were strong on history; the Saxons were much stronger on unwritten lore. Once the Romans finally withdrew their protective legions from Britain, the marauders – Saxons, Picts and Scots especially – poured in, the Saxons from the east, the rest from the north.

Since it was the barbarians who eventually held sway, it is their version of how it happened that has come down to us today, not as unarguable history but as hand-me-down lore. It is a tale of how King Vortigern of Kent invited two Jute chieftains (leaders of one of the many related but different groups we now class together as Saxons) to come and settle in Kent. The chieftains were called Hengist and Horsa, brothers who agreed to fight for Vortigern against the Picts, who were raiding down to the very northern frontier of his kingdom, in return for a grant of land in the Isle of Thanet.

Traditionally, the Jute settlers came in 449, settled in Thanet very happily and at once sent home for more of their tribe. It must have been rather like the migration of the land-hungry settlers into the American west during the nineteenth century.

For a while it was all very chummy, with Vortigern falling in love with and marrying Hengist's daughter, the fair Rowena, and the Jutes daring anyone else to trespass on what was now, at least in part, their territory. Unfortunately, though, the Jutes soon over-populated Thanet and began to cast envious eyes on some of the other good land in the rest of the kingdom. By 455 they had made up their minds that, if they were going to fight for any land, it might as well be their own, and they broke out of Thanet and began to move north and west across the rest of Vortigern's kingdom.

There was one particularly great battle at Aylesford, when many men on both sides were killed, including Horsa and Vortigern's son, Catigern, who are said to have engaged in mutually fatal single combat.

But the dominance of the Saxons did not bring peace. The raids from beyond the seas continued, and there were constant battles with neighbours on the mainland. In 773 – the year in which, we learn, a fiery crucifix appeared in the heavens after sunset one day – there was a great battle between Mercians and Kentish Men at Otford. Kent won, but in 798 Cenwulf of Mercia took revenge, ravaging the kingdom and taking King Praen off in fetters to have his eyes put out and his hands cut off. Kent was subject to Mercian rule after that and was never again the dominant kingdom it had once been.

It was probably in the early 830s that the Danes began to add their bloody chapter to Kentish lore. At first, at any rate, the Danes had no territorial ambitions in England; they came simply to plunder the riches of the many abbeys and monasteries, including their fat cattle and lush crops, and were well enough contented with the historically familiar role in which they have been cast, as revellers in pillaging, burning and raping.

Beginning with a raid on the Isle of Sheppey, by the 840s they were regularly raiding East Kent, and by 850/51 they felt sufficiently at home in Thanet to spend the winter there rather than following previous custom and passing the winter in traditional Norse style in their homeland. They came that year with no fewer than 350 ships, sailing into the Thames and the Medway, sacking Canterbury and London after winning what history now generally accepts as the first English naval battle.

The tactics which King Alfred the Great perfected for combatting the Danish invasion was to hit and run, wreaking what havoc he could among the Danes' supply lines and generally making it as difficult as possible for them to get a secure foothold in the country.

It worked well enough, too, and the Danes found better rewards for their own kind of warfare on the other side of the Channel, where they spread along the coast and evolved (cutting a long story very short) into the Normans, who in 1066 either failed to invade Kent near New Romney and had to go further along the coast to Pevensey in Sussex or else lost a small part of their invasion force which landed in Kent by mistake and was massacred by the local Saxons.

Either way, the landing and first battle actually took place near Hastings, and the Kentish Men were, again traditionally, in the front line of King Harold's army there. Many of them were killed or were still struggling home again when William's Normans marched eastwards along the coast and descended upon Dover to teach that town a very sharp lesson indeed about what happened to slayers of Norman invaders.

William then led his fortune-hunting adventurers inland towards London, turning west to take Winchester before returning to cross the Thames at Wallingford and so taking London from the rear without a fight.

The Norman Conquest did bring a sort of peace again. It was a different quality of peace from that which the Romans had created a thousand years before, and Kent was soon in the front line again when French contenders for the English throne began to press their claims.

The Cinque Ports led a long-running feud with Bayonne in Aquitaine, which was part of the English kingdom, and also with Normandy, which, after it was lost to the French by King John at the beginning of the thirteenth century, was not. Wars were frequent and usually took the form of raids. French portsmen would raid English Channel ports and towns and carry off whatever booty they could lay their hands on, and then the English would replay the visit and take their revenge – and so on.

The Cinque Ports lost no time, once William wore the crown, in asserting that they held their rights from Edward the Confessor and were, therefore, entitled to keep them. Modern historians are inclined to think the wily portsmen exercised a native opportunism and claimed new rights while the going was good. Certainly the collective name for the ports did not come into use before the reign of Henry II in the twelfth century, and they were not fully recognized as a Confederation, with some of the legal standing of a shire, until charters of Henry III and Edward I gave them that recognition.

In 1217 the French Dauphin was in Kent waiting for reinforcements for his planned march on London. The French fleet bringing those reinforcements, commanded by a renegade English monk called Eustace, was in the Channel on St Bartholomew's Day (24 August) when the Cinque Ports fleet under Hubert de Burgh, Constable of Dover Castle, sailed out to meet them. The English fleet was smaller – a recurring feature of English maritime lore, incidentally! – but its commander was more cunning. He manoeuvred to windward of the French and had his men toss quicklime into the wind so that the foreigners were blinded and fell easy prey to the English boarders. Eustace was found and beheaded summarily in his own flagship, the head afterwards being taken to Canterbury to be paraded through the streets on a pole in triumph.

As a result of that fairly unchivalrous but highly effective ploy, the Dauphin signed a peace treaty and went home. But the fighting with the French went on, and the Cinque Ports featured large in much of it.

In 1297 Edward I prepared an expedition to France using both Cinque Ports and east-coast ships based on Yarmouth in Norfolk. Now the south- and east-coast men were old rivals. One of the reasons for that was that among the rights claimed by the Kent men was that of landing and selling herring catches at Yarmouth. That was all right until the practice led to the development of the town of Yarmouth, whose own fishermen began to object to the strangers sharing their own home market when there was no reciprocal arrangement that could have suited the Yarmouth men. There were frequent fights between the two factions, and as soon as Edward I's army was landed at Sluys, the Yarmouth and the Cinque Ports men fell to fighting each other. The Ports won. In fact, Yarmouth lost 17 ships burnt and 12 taken and plundered, and 165 of their men were killed. The feud, incidentally, went on well into the next century.

In 1457 four thousand Frenchmen made a surprise landing at Sandwich and pillaged the town. They murdered the mayor, among others, an event that is still remembered today every time the present mayor dons his uniquely black robe of mourning for those ceremonial occasions when other mayors put on their scarlet and crimson.

After that, war – as distinct from civil disturbance – gradually moved east of Kent onto the continental mainland. The War of the Roses, although fought on English soil, left the county virtually undisturbed, although it took its toll of Kentish noblemen.

Kent ports provided ships to fight the Spanish Armada, and they also did good business servicing Drake's fleet in the Channel. After the English fireships had flushed the Spaniards out of Calais and seen them off on the long way home via North Scotland and the Irish Sea, the Kent ports were filled with sick and dying seamen, many of whom died on the streets.

The next major taste of conflict for Kent after that was in 1667, when the Dutch fleet under Admiral de Ruyter sailed into the Medway, sacking Sheerness and burning several ships of the English fleet at Chatham. Diarist John Evelyn sounded near to tears when he wrote that it was as dreadful a spectacle as ever any Englishman saw. It is an historic episode about which Kentish lore keeps somewhat ruefully silent.

The Civil War brought several clashes between Royalists and Parliamentarians in different parts of Kent, notably at the Battle of Maidstone in 1648 after an army of seven thousand Parliamentarians under General Fairfax marched on the town. The Royalist Earl of Norwich had mustered some ten thousand men on Penenden Heath, the ancient assembly-point for Kentish loyalists, just outside the county town, but Fairfax's men crossed the Medway and took the town piecemeal after bitter hand-to-hand street fighting and praiseworthy bravery in the face of cannon turned on them by the Maidstone Royalists. Royalist casualties in that battle were said to be three hundred killed and fourteen hundred taken prisoner, and they lost a huge quantity of arms and ammunition, too.

After the battle, Fairfax marched on Rochester, but the Royalists were gone from there by the time he arrived, so he turned back to East Kent, and the Kentish Royalist rising ended with the fall of Sandown Castle on 5 September, some five months after it began.

There were, of course, other battles on Kentish soil. One of the saddest, perhaps, has become known as the Battle of Bossenden Wood, in 1838. The events that led to that tragic little fracas began in 1832 when a man calling himself Count Rothschild stayed in a Canterbury inn. He was really plain John Nichols Thom of Cornwall, an eccentric who nevertheless undoubtedly had 'a way with him'. While he was in Canterbury, he 'disclosed' himself as Sir William Honeywood Courtenay and claimed he had already lived for two thousand years. He twice stood for Parliament in Canterbury and during elections was prone to subduing hecklers with a drawn sword.

His behaviour earned him four years in Barming asylum, near Maidstone, but his father petitioned Queen Victoria for his release, and he went back to Canterbury, where he claimed to be the reincarnation of Christ and attracted a number of 'disciples'. Riding a white horse, he went on a recruiting tour of the area, on the Canterbury side of Sittingbourne, and it was during that tour that a farmer complained about this madman who had lured his workers from their fields.

As a result of that complaint, a constable was sent out from Canterbury to arrest Thom. The constable's brother, who went with him, confronted Thom and was killed with a bullet from Thom's pistol. The murderer at once celebrated the killing by administering Holy Communion to his faithful flock and promising them a revolution that would share out the great estates and give them all forty acres of land each. He threatened deserters from his pathetic little army with terrible fates, and they all stayed with him as a major and a hundred men of the 45th Foot sent by a Canterbury Justice came to quell the rising.

There was a battle – though hardly worth the name – in Bossenden Wood at Dunkirk, between Canterbury and Faversham, during which a lieutenant was shot by Courtenay (Thom), and altogether eight people, including Thom, died in the fight.

That much is history. Local lore contends that Thom was buried and lies still in the little churchyard at nearby Hernhill, in an unmarked and now lost grave. The reason the grave was not marked was that the authorities feared the dead man's adherents might try to 'resurrect' him, and it must be admitted now that no one can be sure that none of them ever did, for no record of where the grave was remains.

Napoleon, the Kaiser and Hitler all contributed to Kentish war lore in some measure, but before we reach modern times perhaps this is the right place to consider the regimental lore of the two county regiments, now no more, they having been amalgamated and absorbed into the Queen's Regiment, where only the lore remains as their most lasting memorial.

The oldest of the two was the Buffs, which became particularly associated with East Kent after 1779. The regiment began a three-hundred-year tradition in 1572 as City of London volunteers who went to the Low Countries to help keep the Spanish at a comfortable arm's length from England.

It was because of that that the regiment was originally called the Holland Regiment, and it became commonly known as the Buffs because of the colour of the uniform facings. Years later, the nickname was adopted formally as the full and proper title of the regiment. Later still, it won other nicknames, including 'the Nut Crackers' and 'the Resurrectionists' – the last earned by successfully recruiting back to full strength after heavy losses during the Peninsula War. It became the Third Regiment of Foot, one of the most senior in the British Army.

General Sir Jeffrey Amherst, who distinguished himself against the French in Canada and whose home was near Sevenoaks, was once Colonel of the Buffs, before Major General Style of Wateringbury took over the post in 1779. It was then that the special relationship with East Kent began, although it was not formalized until much later.

'Steady the Buffs!' became something of a catchphrase throughout the army whenever there was a need for fighting men to stand firm against difficult odds. The phrase was said to have been born in 1858 in Malta when Adjutant Cotter, a former sergeant-major with the 1st Royal North British (later Scots) Fusiliers rallied recruits with the call: 'Steady the Buffs – the Fusiliers are watching you!'

There was a special relationship between the Buffs and the Royal Fusiliers from 1811 onwards, as a result of an incident that occurred during the Peninsula War.

It happened near Albuhera, where the Buffs met an attack by Marshal Soult's forces and threw them back during a hailstorm which reduced visibility to nil, so that the Englishmen were not prepared when French hussars and Polish lancers launched a counter-attack upon their flank. There was fierce hand-to-hand fighting, during which the regimental colours were lost and Ensign Walsh, who held the King's Colour, was struck down.

A certain Lieutenant Matthew Latham fought his way to the side of the fallen ensign and snatched up the colour, prepared to defend it with his life. He very nearly had to. His face was split open by a sabre, and one arm was completely severed, and although he had lost his own sword, he hugged the colour to his body as he went down under the hacking attack.

Later that day, the regimental colour was recovered by a sergeant of the Royal Fusiliers and returned to the Buffs. After that, the two regiments always shared honorary membership of each other's messes.

Latham was found at the end of the battle with the King's Colour, bloody but safe, inside his tunic. He was not dead, and after surgery, which was paid for personally by the Prince of Wales, he was awarded a special gold medal and continued to serve with the regiment until 1827, when he retired and married and fathered nine children before he died in 1855.

Lieutenant Latham's bravery in defence of the King's Colour that day is the subject of a very handsome silver table centrepiece showing a mounted French officer trying to wrest the flag from the severely wounded Lieutenant Latham, and it is the pride of all the regimental silver.

Later in the same campaign, the Buffs' regimental mascot during the invasion of France from Spain was a bull-terrier called Crib. He distinguished himself particularly by killing (in what I suppose must be called single combat) a French poodle that was the mascot of one of the French regiments. When he died, Crib was rewarded with his own tombstone in the church of St Martin's in the Strand in London.

Probably the most famous of all the stories told about the Buffs arose from an incident in 1860 when the regiment was among troops sent to rescue British and French traders in China. During the march, they were attacked by Tartar horsemen, and although they beat them off, the retreating Tartars took prisoner some stragglers, including Buffs Private John Moyse, who was travelling in the rear of the column with the division's grog carts.

The prisoners were taken to a Tartar mandarin, before whom they were ordered to kowtow or be beheaded. According to the legend, Moyse drew himself up and replied: 'I'm a Man of Kent. I'm not bowing and scraping in front of any heathen.' His pride lost him his head but earned him immortality in a poem by Sir Francis Doyle, entitled 'The Private of the Buffs'.

In fact, sceptical regimental historians have since thrown doubt upon the likelihood that the story was true. It has been suggested

that Private Moyse was not even a Man of Kent at all but a Scot
recruited into the regiment during a period it spent north of the
border. He had, it seems, once been a colour sergeant but had
been demoted by court martial, which was how he came to be
among the grog-cart stragglers in the first place, and it is even
suggested that he and others with him had been helping themselves pretty liberally from the grog cart and were therefore not
able to defend themselves when the Tartar horsemen descended
upon them. Whether or not Private Moyse did, in fact, defy the
order to kowtow, in whatever terms, we cannot now be sure.

It is rather sad, in one sense, that truth must mar the lore, but,
of course, historians are well known for the delight they take in
spoiling a good story with the truth.

The other Kent regiment was the Queen's Own Royal West
Kent Regiment – the old 50th, which dated its origins back,
though indirectly, to 1743. After the former 50th and 51st regiments were disbanded in 1756, the old 52nd was renumbered the
50th, and it was that regiment which became, in time, the Royal
West Kents.

Among their nicknames were 'The Devil's Royals', 'The Blind
Half-hundred' and 'The Dirty Half-hundred' – the half-hundred
referring in each case not to the number of men but to the
regimental number 50.

During the Peninsula War, the 50th marched to meet Lieuten-
ant-General Sir John Moore's forces as Salamanca under the
command of Major the Honourable Charles Stanhope. It was
during that march that they became known as 'the Dirty Half-
hundred', because the black dye of their uniform cuffs streaked
their faces when they wiped away the sweat.

Later they were honoured with the title of 'The 50th (Queen's
Own) Regiment', the queen whose own they were being William
IV's Queen Adelaide, and in recognition of the royal patronage
the black uniform facings were replaced with new ones of royal
blue.

The regiment earned its 'Blind Half-hundred' nickname during
the Egyptian campaign in 1801, when most of the men suffered
from an eye complaint caused by desert dust. Legend has it that,
as a result of the complaint, men of the regiment once charged a
field of red cabbages, mistaking them for the enemy. The story is
almost certainly not true and was probably a slanderous joke
made by some other regimental wit, but the Queen's Own

adopted it as an illustration of their readiness to tackle any-thing.

The regiment logged a respectable body of lore of its own, and one of the best stories concerns an incident in the Middle East in 1917.

Apparently, two Territorial privates of General Sir Edmund Allenby's army in the desert outside Jerusalem were out looking for water for a brew-up, when they were approached by a little procession under a white flag. The procession turned out to include the hereditary Mayor of Jerusalem, who solemnly hand-ed over the keys of the city to the two astonished privates, who could not understand a word that was being said to them, nor make out quite what was going on. However, they recognized that they were being presented with something or other, so they drew themselves up, saluted and shook hands with becoming gravity, and then went off about the really important business of the day – finding that water so they could make a cup of tea.

They kept the keys, which they thought were quite nice, as keys go, if a bit useless without any labels to tell them what doors they would open. It was not until after Allenby had made his triumphal entry into Jerusalem some time later that he learned that the keys had already been handed over officially and with some little ceremony to two of his privates who hadn't even bothered to report the incident.

The general's exact words when he heard the news have not passed into regimental lore – and perhaps that is just as well.

Incidentally the first Victoria Cross was won during the Crimean War by Lieutenant (later Rear-Admiral) Charles Lucas of Tunbridge Wells. He was eventually buried at Mereworth.

Despite their war-like associations, castles were not merely fortresses. Much of the time they were homes and centres of an administrative system. Nevertheless, much of the lore that has encrusted their ancient stones over the centuries has been the result of conflict of one kind or another.

Leeds Castle, near Maidstone, is sometimes called the loveliest castle in the world. In its moated setting amid the rolling country-side of one of the loveliest parts of a lovely county, Leeds is certainly picturesque enough for any picture postcard, chocolate box or guidebook cover. But, like many another castle, it has seen its uglier moments, too.

One of the ugliest was the day in October 1321 when Queen

Isabella (the Fair) was on a pilgrimage to Canterbury with a substantial retinue including men-at-arms, and she stopped at Leeds to demand lodgings for herself and her party in the castle.

Until her husband, Edward II, exchanged Leeds Castle for a Shropshire manor owned by Bartholomew de Badlesmere, the castle had been in royal ownership for two hundred years. It had become customary for kings to give it to their queens, as a result of which it had become known as 'the Ladies' Castle', and no doubt Isabella still regarded it as more hers than his when he decided upon the exchange, and probably resented his decision.

However, the new owner, de Badlesmere, who had been the King's steward at Leeds before he became its owner, was out of the county on business in the north of England, and the Queen's demands had to be answered by his wife and the new steward, Walter Colepeper. Colepeper took it upon himself to declare that, without instructions from his master, he could not offer the Queen the hospitality she demanded, and he closed the castle doors on the royal entourage.

The Queen was furious. She gave orders for her men to assault the castle and force an entry, but the castle was proof against anything so small a force could do, and Isabella had to withdraw and seek lodgings elsewhere.

But she took the first opportunity that presented itself to complain to the King about the way she had been insulted at Leeds, and he – perhaps over-reacting to compensate for the way he had displeased his wife by disposing of the castle – summoned the Sheriffs of Essex, Hampshire, Surry and Sussex to conscript every man between the ages of sixteen and sixty from their counties and assemble before Leeds Castle by Friday 23 October. At the same time, a message went to the Sheriff of Kent, telling him to have his own men at Leeds on 20 October, to make ready for the arrival of the others, who would be joined by the King himself on the Friday.

News of the royal siege reached de Badlesmere, who enlisted the help of the Archbishop of Canterbury, the Bishop of London and others to ask the King to raise the siege and let Parliament settle the dispute. But Edward dismissed the peacemakers impatiently and sat tight on the shores of the artificial lake that moated the castle.

Well, although the castle was proof against direct attack, it was not sufficiently prepared for a long siege, and on 1 November the garrison surrendered. The King's justice was swift and conclusive. Walter Colepeper and twelve others were executed, hung from the battlements of the castle they had defended so loyally for their absent master. Lady Badlesmere and her children were sent to the Tower of London, and the family jewels and possessions were handed to the Abbot of Leeds.

Bartholomew de Badlesmere, rather wisely in the circumstances, stayed in the north, but he was eventually captured and brought south, where he was charged with treason, found guilty and executed. His head was spiked over the Borough Gate at Canterbury. Leeds Castle was taken back by the King and was later owned by Anne of Bohemia, first wife of Richard II, and then by Catherine de Valois, Henry V's queen, continuing the tradition of the lovely little Ladies' Castle in Kent.

The castle has been the prison of Richard II after he was deposed by Henry IV, of Joanna of Navarre (accused of trying to kill her stepson, Henry V, by witchcraft) and in 1441 of Eleanor, Duchess of Gloucester, accused of witchcraft and/or treason.

In 1665 war again touched Leeds, when part of it was leased to the Government to be used as a prison for six hundred French and Dutch prisoners of war.

Rochester Castle has certainly been in the wars. Indeed, whenever there was trouble in Kent, Rochester always seemed to feature in it.

King John, having provoked the barons to rebellion by his refusal to abide by the conditions written into Magna Carta, joined in the feuding that followed and in June 1215 was to be found at Rochester directing the long siege of the castle there. The castle finally fell when the King's men tunnelled under the south-east corner of the keep and breached it. The corner was afterwards rebuilt in a stronger, rounded form – the form in which it is still to be seen today.

In 1450, after the rebel Jack Cade had been pardoned by King Henry VI for his revolting behaviour, he returned to Kent apparently with his energies unspent and attacked Rochester Castle. The rather pointless gesture cost him his pardon, and he was killed four days later by Alexander Iden, Sheriff of Kent and Sussex.

In 1554 Rochester Castle was again under attack, this time by supporters of Sir Thomas Wyatt's rebellion to prevent the marriage of Queen Mary to Philip of Spain. This time, the castle actually fell to the rebels, only to be restored to its former owner after Wyatt lost his head on Tower Hill.

But, of course, Dover Castle has always been the premier castle among all of those in Kent, and, if only because of the length of its known history, it is inevitable that it holds pride of place in any recitation of the lore of the castles of the county.

The building of the present castle began in 1168, and it was the scene of several warlike incidents very early on. The earlier castle had surrendered, in 1138, to the forces of King Stephen under a mercenary captain from Flanders, William de Ypres, who later became Earl of Kent.

Towards the end of King John's reign, the French Dauphin was invited to come to England by some of the barons, and he landed at Stonar and marched inland. He took the castles of Canterbury and Rochester and sent messages demanding the surrender of Dover Castle, which was being held by Hubert de Burgh, Justiciar of England and Constable of Dover.

He was not a man to whom surrender came easily, and he refused point-blank, replying: 'Let not Louis [the Dauphin] hope that I will surrender as long as I draw breath. Never will I yield to French aliens this castle which is the very key and gate of England.'

Stirring stuff – and, indeed, de Burgh backed them with action just as soon as he had an opportunity, destroying a French fleet bringing reinforcements to the Dauphin in England, and forcing the Dauphin to sign a peace treaty and withdraw.

There are stories relating to the actual building of Dover Castle, too, which are certainly not history but which live on in lore. One of them concerns Peverell's Tower, which kept collapsing while it was being built, and in the end, to propitiate the evil spirts which were blamed, an old woman and her dog were walled up in one of the walls. The old woman cursed the chief mason so heartily as she was being entombed that, when the building was completed, he fell to his death from the very top of the tower.

Kent played a major role in World War II, both as a battle-ground in itself and as the nearest port of England to occupied France. It was from the Kent Channel ports that many of the Expeditionary Force left for France in 1939; it was to Kent that thousands of rescued soldiers came aboard the famous little ships flotilla that ferried them back from the Dunkirk beaches; it was in the skies over Kent that the Battle of Britain was fought in 1940 and which became the killing ground for the V1 'Doodlebug' flying bombs later on; and it was from Kent that some of the D-day invasion forces began the business of liberating the occupied countries as the war drew to its close.

No wonder that war left a great deal of lore littering the county, some of which has since been confirmed as genuine history, but some of which has not.

Contributors to that lore were Winnie and Pooh, two fourteen-inch ex-naval guns which were installed, amid great secrecy, at St Margarets-at-Cliffe, not far from Dover itself. Winnie was named in honour of the nickname by which Prime Minister Winston Churchill was almost universally known. Pooh was so named because it went naturally with Winnie, thanks to A. A. Milne and his creation of Christopher Robin and his friends.

Winnie fired her first shell across the Channel on 28 August, 1940, and the Battery Commander telephoned Churchill direct with the news.

'Winnie fired her first shot today and scored a direct hit,' he said.

With characteristic bluntness, the Prime Minister demanded: 'Direct hit on what?'

'On France!' was the reply.

Well – that's the story, anyway.

The oddities of bomb-blast created their own lore, and everyone had his own story to tell of people stripped naked but otherwise unharmed; of cage-birds surviving among ruins in which everyone else was killed; of vehicles lifted off the ground and turned round so that they faced the other way without suffering any damage at all.

A news blackout kept most of these and many other stories out of the newspapers at the time. A great deal of lore was built up around secret behaviour of all kinds, hints and rumours of which leaked into common knowledge, frequently inaccurately, exaggerated and distorted, and sometimes simply untrue. Some were written down; most were not. They all contributed generously to the lore of the period.

One such story that was certainly not true was that which became current in Dover and further inland during the tense days of 1940: that the enemy had actually dug a Channel tunnel to the English coast and that it only needed to be completed by the excavation of a few more yards of chalk to spew an invasion army into the heart of Kent. It sounds pretty silly now, especially in view of all that has happened with regard to the real Channel tunnel in more recent times, but in 1940 such stories were not dismissed without some doubts remaining.

On the other hand, stories of plans to engulf any surface invaders in a sea of flame by pouring oil onto the sea and setting light to it were actually encouraged by our own Government in order to make sure that the Germans knew about the idea and hesitated to risk an invasion. After the war it became known that, in fact, only a few short lengths of beach at Walmer, Ramsgate and Dover were protected in this way, and they would certainly not have been enough to stem a determined invasion along a wide area of the coastline.

Spy stories were popular in those Dad's Army days, too. One of many stories told about spies, real and imagined, concerned a French-speaking German and a Dutchman who landed at Dungeness early in the war, assigned to set up a spy network in the south of England. They failed after the Dutchman, speaking good English, tried to buy cider at a pub in Lydd at breakfast time. The landlady told him he would have to come back at ten o'clock, and when he did, the police and military were waiting for him. Who says our licensing laws are all bad?

During August 1940 German flyers began to call Kent 'Hell's Corner' (or 'Hellfire Corner') because this was where they encountered the fiercest opposition on their way to bomb London. The name won a place in Kentish history, and Kent took a great deal of pride in it.

Many were the stories told about flyers during those days. Again, few of them were ever committed to paper. One that did earn a place in the records, though, concerned Flying Officer Paul le Brougtel, who was shot down off St Margaret's Bay in August 1940. Lifeboat Coxswain 'Sinbad' Price was on air-sea rescue patrol when he glimpsed the momentary flash of the sun from the dial of the 'ditched' pilot's wrist watch. Dashing to the rescue, he was just in time to snatch the airman from the sea before he became unconscious and unable to wave his hand any more. If that had happened, he would almost certainly have drifted out of reach of rescue and died.

Then there was Pilot Officer Paddy Stevenson, who found himself engaged by two German Dorniers after he had run out of ammunition. Unwilling to be shot down without a fight of any kind, he turned and rammed the two enemy aircraft with his right and left wings, bringing both down. His own plane, of course, was crippled, and he had to parachute to safety – landing in the grounds of a mental hospital.

Whenever that one was told in the mess, the one about Pilot Officer Richard Hillery capped it. Hillery was shot down over Lympne near Ashford in August 1940. He baled out and landed in the middle of a cocktail party being given by a local brigadier.

Stories like these were legion at the time. Many of them have been told; some are undoubtedly true; some might be true. Quite a lot almost certainly are not.

But odd things happen in wars, and it is never altogether wise to dismiss any of the stories as totally without foundation. They are too unsubstantiated ever to be accepted as recorded history, but much too colourful to forget. They are, in fact, quintessentially, war lore.

8

Spirits of the Lore

Kent may not be any more haunted by ghosts than anywhere else in Great Britain, but one of its villages certainly claims to be. Pluckley lies some six or seven miles north-west of Ashford and might very well be dismissed with the briefest of mentions in the guidebooks were it not for its reputation as the most haunted village in England.

In the last five hundred years, at least a dozen ghosts have wafted their way into local lore, and, although it becomes more and more difficult to find anyone who will admit to having seen or heard any of them, nobody actually rushes to disclaim them all.

For centuries the Dering family owned most of Pluckley, and several of the local legends feature former Dering squires and their families. Like the mysterious Red Lady, probably the most frequently seen of all the Pluckley ghosts. She was the wife of a fifteenth-century Dering whose child died tragically, and now, dressed in a flowing red gown, the distraught mother still walks both the family chapel in St Nicholas' Church and the church-yard, wandering among the headstones poignantly searching for her baby's grave – or so they say.

The old Dering home, Surrenden Dering, was burnt to the ground in 1950, but the site is still said to be haunted by another former Dering, this one known as the White Lady.

According to the legend, she was the exceptionally beautiful wife of one of the squires, and she died while still very young. Her husband was heartbroken and could not bear to think that such beauty should follow the laws of nature and return to dust, so he had her serving ladies dress the body in fine clothes, and he placed on the dead breast a red rose, emblem of his enduring love. Then he had the body placed in three lead coffins, one inside another, and all three encased in an oak casket which was laid in the family vault beneath the Dering Chapel in the church.

Whether or not his efforts to preserve his dead wife's mortal beauty were successful, they did not, evidently, help her to rest in peace, for now she walks, from time to time, through the old churchyard, but more often in or near the site of the former mansion, clutching to her breast the single red rose that was her doting husband's last tribute to her beauty, centuries ago.

Over the years there have been reports of a ghostly white dog, flickering lights and inexplicable hammering noises coming from the Dering Chapel, and sometimes the sound of a woman's voice is said to have been heard echoing between the old walls.

But the Dering family has no monopoly of the hauntings on this extensive estate.

In Dicky Buss's Lane, opposite the Black Horse Inn (itself distinguished more for the spirit of its hospitality and particularly for its catering than for any spectral phenomena), a former schoolmaster periodically goes through the ghostly motions of that sad day when he committed suicide by hanging himself there.

A phantom soldier is said to march doggedly through a wood in the parish, and a ghostly miller revisits the remains of the village mill when the moon is full. A long-departed resident of Rose Court can still be heard calling spectrally to her equally long-departed dogs, and in the grounds of a house called Greystones a monk has been seen.

Other Pluckley ghosts include an old tramp who used to frequent the village during his lifetime, and a young girl who died from eating poison ivy; and a young man, generally judged to have been a nineteenth-century suicide, has been seen in one of the bedrooms of the five-hundred-year-old Elvery Farmhouse, which was once part of the old Dering estate.

Oh – and a scream occasionally rings out from the century old brickfield known as the Old Clayhole, where a workman is said to have been killed in a tragic accident many years ago.

That is not the last of the Pluckley ghosts, though. There is an old gipsy watercress-seller who accidentally burned herself to death when she fell asleep among some hay while she was smoking her clay pipe; and a highwayman who seems unable to accept that his lawless days are now part of the village's lorefulness.

The story about him tells how he used to hide in a hollow oak at a local crossroads and leap out with his demands to travellers to stand and deliver. One traveller, though, had heard about this particular example of local enterprise and, being an enterprising man himself, plunged his sword through the tree's oaken shell as he passed, pinning the highwayman to the inside of the trunk before he could make his usual pounce.

The crossroads, incidentally, is still known locally as Fright Corner.

Finally – if, indeed, one can ever be sure of reaching finality on the subject of ghosts in Pluckley – a phantom coach drawn by phantom horses has been known to career through the village main street by night, though not, I believe, for many years.

But, however it might seem from that little catalogue, not all the ghosts of Kent have congregated in Pluckley by any means. Indeed, some of the others are better known, for one reason or another.

One of the best known, perhaps, is the Blue Bell Hill ghost, which has been the subject of investigation and conjecture by national newsmen and psychic researchers more than once. Blue Bell Hill is the steep dual-carriageway link between Maidstone and the Medway Towns, and the ghost is said to be that of a young girl who died in a road crash there in 1965.

She was, the story goes, one of three girls, all in their early twenties, who were killed in the same accident one night. They had spent the evening with a friend who was to be married at the weekend, and they had been trying on dresses they would wear to the wedding. One of the girls was to be a bridesmaid. Later that evening, they all agreed to go with the bride-to-be to meet her fiancé in a pub, but as they drove together in one car up Blue Bell Hill, the car spun off the road, and three of the four girls were killed.

Since then there have been recurring reports of a ghostly hitch-hiker at the side of the road. Most of the reports tell of drivers who have stopped to offer her a lift. She has got into the car, usually in the back seat, and then, after the car has resumed its journey, the driver has found that he is alone in it again.

One driver dashed to Rochester police station late one night after trying unsuccessfully to wave down other passing motorists, and reported that he had hit a pedestrian on the hill. He told policemen he had left her lying at the roadside, covered with his car rug, thinking he could get help more quickly by driving straight to the police station than by trying to knock up a householder with a telephone at that hour.

Police raced to the spot. They found the car rug but no trace of the girl, and after a search of the area failed to bring to light any clues to what had really happened, they told the shocked motorist that he must have become the latest of a number of people who had encountered the phantom hitch-hiker.

Another famous Kent spectre is that which haunts Bloor Lane at Rainham, east of Gillingham. In Tudor times, Bloor's Place at the Lower Rainham end of the lane was the home of Christopher Bloor, an infamous womanizer whose life was constantly threatened by jealous and irate husbands. One night – legend has it – he was driving home in his coach, probably from one of his assignations, when the coach was waylaid by townspeople who dragged him out and cut off his head on the spot. They then set up the severed head on a pole outside Rainham church, as a warning to any other young rakes who might be tempted by the attractions of the local wives to carry on where Bloor perforce left off.

Then they sent the coach and the headless body back to Bloor's Place.

Now, periodically, there are stories of a coach drawn by a headless horse and driven by a headless coachman, with a headless footman in attendance, leaving Rainham church for where Bloor's Place used to be, at midnight. Inside the coach sits Christopher Bloor, his head under his arm, but when the coach enters the Bloor's Place grounds, the whole apparition always vanishes. The journey is supposed to have been made by the ghostly Bloor to retrieve his spiked head from outside the church.

Another phantom coach haunts Stone Street, the B2068, which runs for ten miles or so with Roman straightness between Canterbury and Hythe. This coach is supposed to be drawn by four black horses breathing smoke and fire, and driven by a spectral coachman with his head in his lap. The story seems to be rooted, however loosely, in a sixteen-year-old's diary entry telling how, while driving home from a party one night with her brothers and sisters, their coach overturned and the passengers were spilled out into Stone Street.

The diary was kept in the eighteenth century by the daughter of the decidedly eccentric Lord Rokeby. His eccentricity took the form of refusing to cut any of the shrubs or even the grass on his estate. He is also said to have had two baths, one of marble for weekdays and a golden one for Sundays, and to have spent most of his time in one or other of them, emerging occasionally to wander, naked, through his necessarily somewhat overgrown park. As he also refused to cut his beard, which hung to his knees, perhaps he was able to indulge that last eccentricity without offending anyone.

A ghost achieved official recognition during World War II by appearing to one of the guards on duty at Chatham Dockyard one night. The dockyard logbook includes an entry: 'Ghost reported seen during the middle watch.' The apparition was said to have been that of a ghostly peg-legged sailor of Nelson's time, and it is thought that he was murdered by French prisoners escaping, perhaps, from one of the prison hulks in the Medway during that period.

Customers of pubs who tell of encounters with ghosts on the premises must not be offended if their tales are heard with a certain amount of scepticism. Nevertheless, many pubs do claim to be haunted. One which lends itself rather well to spectral visitations is the old Shipwrights' Arms at Hollow Shore, an arm of Faversham Creek. There the ghost, reported by both the wife of a former licensee and several of their customers, was said to be that of an old man with staring eyes.

The Coopers Arms in Rochester claims it may be the oldest pub in Kent because it was once part of an eleventh-century priory. There is a story that one of the monks was once walled up there and that his ghost still walks the premises from time to time.

Also in Rochester, the Good Companions Club became famous as the happy haunting-ground of the ghost of a love-sick sailor called Edwin Wilkes. According to the legend, he was murdered in 1723 by his wife's lover and thrown down a well. Could be: there was once a well, before it was boarded over, in one corner of the club bar.

Then, still in Rochester, there is a window in a once-secret room of Eastgate House which was only rediscovered this century, which is said sometimes to frame a ghostly head which peers out and then disappears. A ghostly monk is said to walk through the Vines, an open space behind the cathedral close where the monks once had their vineyard.

One of the saddest of Rochester's ghosts is surely that of the lovely Lady Blanche, who was killed by an arrow accidentally shot by her lover during a siege on Good Friday 1264.

The castle was besieged by Simon de Montfort, Earl of Leicester. Inside, defending the stronghold, was Ralph de Capo, who had with him in the castle the lovely Lady Blanche de Warenne.

One of de Montfort's men was Gilbert de Clare, rejected suitor of Lady Blanche, and when the siege was raised, de Capo pursued the retreating de Montfort army. De Clare, disguising himself as de Capo, went into the castle and sought out Lady Blanche up on the battlements, where, no doubt, she was anxiously following the derring-do of her beloved. De Capo, happening to look back (let's suppose he wanted to be sure he still had the undivided attention of the lady), saw her struggling for her virtue in the arms of the dastardly de Clare. Enraged, the lover seized a crossbow and loosed a bolt at the usurper. Unhappily, though, the bolt glanced off de Clare's armour and killed Blanche.

Incidentally, there are other versions of the same story, including one in which Lady Blanche hurled herself from the battlements rather than submit to de Clare. But all versions seem to agree that Lady Blanche, however she left this life, is still doing her best to return to it by haunting the castle battlements.

We have no less an authority than Daniel Defoe to whom to turn for the curious Mrs Veal's apparition. It was during a visit to Canterbury that Defoe heard about this curiosity, and he was so intrigued – or possibly so sure he was on to a good thing, journalistically – that he published a pamphlet titled *A True Relation of the Apparition of one Mrs Veal, the next day after her death, to one Mrs Bargrave, at Canterbury, the 8th September, 1705 – which apparition recommends the Perusal of Drelincourt's Book of Consolations against the Fears of Death.*

With a title like that, you might think, who needs the story? Indeed, there isn't a lot more to the story itself. Apparently, one Saturday, 8 September 1705, a Mrs Veal of Dover visited her friend Mrs Bargrave at her house in Canterbury. Mrs Bargrave thought nothing out of the ordinary about it until she learned that Mrs Veal had in fact died at Dover the day before. When news of the visit – or visitation – became public, it attracted a good deal of attention and even reached the ears of Queen Anne and her consort, Prince George of Denmark, who asked a local expert in matters metaphysical to investigate further for him.

Even that investigation did not bring a great deal more to light, but it seems that Mrs Veal, during her visit to Canterbury, told Mrs Bargrave that she was about to go on a long journey and would Mrs Bargrave please arrange with Mrs Veal's brother to have a tombstone made for their mother's grave, but large enough to have room for Mrs Veal's name as well. Mrs Veal then left, saying that she was going to see a cousin who also lived in Canterbury – and was never seen again.

Inevitably, a city as old as Canterbury can well hold its own (except, perhaps, against Pluckley!) in the matter of ghosts. But none has ever received better publicity than that given to Nell Cook in Richard Barham's *Ingoldsby Legends* of that name.

It was – the Legend tells us – in bluff King Harry's days that a portly canon lived near the Dark Entry leading into Canterbury Cathedral cloisters, where he was well served in matters culinary – and, by implication, in other ways, too – by his cook, Ellen Bean, familiarly known to her employer as Nelly Cook.

As the Legend puts it so becomingly: 'And though her gown was russet brown, their heads grave people shook: They all agreed no Clerk had need of such a pretty Cook.'

Well, one day there arrived at the house a young lady whom the Canon welcomed as his 'dearest niece' but upon whom Nelly Cook looked askew as it came into her mind that 'They were a little less than kin, and rather more than kind.'

Nell tested out her suspicions by secreting a poker and fire-tongs in the lady's bed, and, when they remained there undisturbed for six weeks, Nell concluded that, if the fair visitor was sleeping in any bed at all, it certainly was not her own. Jealousy joined the company in the Canon's house, and Nell baked her speciality, a warden pie, specially doctored, for the couple.

Next morning, when the Canon was nowhere to be found, the monks broke into his house and, searching it, found master and his mistress dead in bed together. Scandal was averted, and the couple were buried together. But from that day on, Nelly Cook, too, disappeared.

Some years later, the Legend goes on, a certain stone slab in the Dark Entry passageway had to be replaced because it was worn, and when the masons took it up, they found a hole, not more than twelve feet deep and barely twelve feet round, in which was a skeleton beside a mouldy piece of kissing-crust from a warden pie. The bones were identified as those of a female, and it was assumed that they were, in fact, those of Nelly Cook, walled up in the well by the monks for poisoning their brother – and to make quite sure she never revealed the truth about the way he had died.

But the Legend does not end there. It goes on to tell how, throughout the year on every Friday night, Nell Cook's spirit roams the Dark Entry, and if anyone should encounter her, he will die within the year, and as proof of that instances the fate of the three masons who found the skeleton: 'Two were hanged on Tyburn tree for murdering of the third.'

It is probably the best – and certainly the best-told – of all Kentish ghost stories, and none the worse for being revealed as a spoof from first to last, by its author.

The village of Boxley, at the foot of the North Downs near Maidstone, is said to be haunted by five different ghosts. One, associated with Boxley House, now a hotel but previously a school and before that a public house, was a butler who supposedly committed suicide there in the 1890s.

Richborough, between Sandwich and Thanet, was in its heyday an important Roman port. The massive ruins of the castle the Romans built there remains today, but since the legions left, Richborough has retreated well inland, and the new shoreline is a busy industrial area. During the Second World War it was a top-secret area, heavily defended and once more well populated with soldiers. Perhaps the atmosphere was conducive to the return of the legionaries, for several soldiers reported seeing cohorts of Roman soldiers marching down to the sea from there.

Others said they watched a duel between a Roman soldier and a Saxon warrior on the nearby seashore. They do not seem to have noted who won.

Lympne Castle is another well-haunted building. Lympne was the Roman Portus Lemanis, one of the Forts of the Saxon Shore when it guarded one branch of the River Rother, the Limen, now vanished since the river changed its course and altered the history of a number of the Romney Marsh coastal towns.

Lympne Castle was built about 1360, overlooking the older Roman castle, the remains of which we know today as Stutfall Castle. One of the ghosts of Lympne is an altogether alarming creature which has been described as having the body of an eagle and the skull of a man, and it is said to fly around the kingpost in the bedroom which once was used by an archdeacon.

A sad-eyed priest used to look down into the Great Hall from a small slit window at the top of the eastern wall, and he was said to have been one of seven Saxon priests who lived there at the time of the Domesday Survey (and so before the present building existed) and who were murdered by person or persons now unknown. The Domesday Book recorded their existence, but four years later they were gone and never heard of again.

Then, in the eastern tower of Lympne Castle, on the site of a one-time Roman watch-tower, a ghostly Roman soldier has been heard thumping up the steps and seen gazing seawards, presumably still on watch for Saxon raiders. The theory is that the soldier so loved the view from the watch-tower that he has not yet been able to bring himself to leave it.

Among the miscellany of ghosts of Kent, Harbourne House and Turks Head at High Halden are both said to have been haunted; there is a White Lady of Chilham; and Dover has its smuggler, Dover Bill.

In a sixteenth-century Faversham house a child was once sent to bed for losing a shoe. During the night, the little girl left her room and, in an effort to appease her parents, searched the house for the missing shoe. During the search she fell down the stairs, broke her neck and died. Years later the tiny shoe was found under oak floorboards where it must have slipped out of sight or, perhaps, children being children, been poked and forgotten about. The childish spirit was said to haunt the house after that.

Not surprisingly, perhaps, the ghost of Anne Boleyn is said to haunt her old family home, Hever Castle, and at Cleve Court, Minster (Isle of Thanet), the wife of a former owner, Lord Carson, the lawyer and politician who died in 1966, was convinced the house was haunted by a Grey Lady who appeared whenever there were children in the house. She believed the spirit was that of the wife of a tyrannical former owner, who kept her childless and locked in her room.

At Chatham, a woman who was murdered on the Lines more than two hundred years ago is still sometimes to be seen, walking her two ghostly dogs there, and Herne Bay Downs are said to be haunted by the ghost of a girl who was loved by two soldiers stationed nearby during the Napoleonic Wars period. The rivals fought a duel over her, and when she tried to stop them, she was killed. Both soldiers were arrested and brought to trial, but neither would accuse the other, and so both were hanged for her murder.

Not far from Sevenoaks is the village of Plaxtol, where you will find the beautifully preserved thirteenth-century manor house of Old Soar. It is haunted by a girl called Jenny who, it is said, lived in one of the estate cottages during the eighteenth century. At Christmas 1775, when Jenny was seventeen years old, the lord of the manor held a great feast for all the local gentry, and Jenny was called in to prepare fresh cream and butter for the guests. While she was at work, the family priest, who was drunk at the time, behaved in a wholly unpriestly manner towards the girl – in fact, not to mince matters since the local legend does not, he raped her.

When Jenny found she was pregnant as a result of this encounter, she went to see the priest, and he suggested that the best solution for everyone would be for her to marry her boyfriend. Feeling, no doubt, that having given that advice he had done all that could be expected of him in the circumstances, the priest left her then, in the family chapel. Alone and not specially reassured, since she knew very well that her boyfriend's affection for her was, at the very least, less ardent than hers for him, she fainted and hit her head on the font, in which she drowned.

It was generally supposed that she had committed suicide, and so she was buried in unconsecrated ground, after the manner of her time, from which she returns to haunt the chapel with strange lights and church music in revenge for the injustice she suffered during her young lifetime.

At Hollingbourne, not far from Maidstone, is a fine Georgian house, the remains of a once E-shaped larger house, Hollingbourne Manor. It is said to be haunted by the ghost of one of the wives of Henry VIII, Catherine Howard, who lived there (according to local lore and no other evidence at all!) until she was fifteen, when she went to Court and started on the path that led her into the King's favour, out of it again and thus to the executioner's block on Tower Hill.

The grounds of Cooling Castle, most of which is now in ruins out there on the seaward edge of the Hoo Peninsula, but which still has a modest occupied part, are said to be haunted by Sir John Oldcastle, one-time owner of the castle and generally supposed to have been the real-life model for Shakespeare's Falstaff.

Oldcastle supported John Wycliff's Lollards, who wanted the riches of the Church to be shared with the poor, and he was ordered to be arrested by the Archbishop. He escaped but was eventually captured, and, on Christmas Day 1417, he was hanged and burned while hanging before the gates of St Giles' Hospital in London, watched by a large crowd of onlookers.

Finally, one ghost which Kent does not, apparently, have after all. The Lady of the Pond. For years before 1939, there was a legend that the pond of Iborden Park, near Biddenden in the Weald of Kent, was haunted by a beautiful young lady in a magnificent ball-gown. The story was told locally of how the lovely foster-daughter of a squire drowned herself there during her eighteenth-birthday ball, after her foster-brother, with whom she was passionately in love, spurned her.

The poor girl's ghost was said to walk round the pond on the anniversary of the tragedy, but in 1939 Mr Frederick Sanders of Chatham, an experienced ghost-hunter by reputation, visited the pond and returned declaring the atmosphere there was exceptionally peaceful and that, in his opinion, there was no ghost.

Ah, well . . .

9

River Lore

All rivers are more or less loreful. Well, of course, most of them have had a very long time indeed to collect tales and legends to be told about them. They were among the first landmarks, the first boundaries, the first highways, always ready-made, and in all of man's history, and even his pre-history, the rivers were there.

Kent has two main rivers of its own. In addition, it shares one of England's greatest rivers, the Thames, the south bank of which has been the northern boundary of the county for centuries. Naturally enough, much of the lore of the Thames is that of Kent, too.

But it is the Medway that is Kent's own premier waterway. From the county's earliest history it has been the Medway that has given Kent its uniquely divided character, with the Men of Kent on the eastern side and the Kentish Men on the west.

The distinction between the two began almost two thousand years ago when the North European migrants we now generally call simply the Saxons began to colonize south-east England. It was a group of Jutes who came to East Kent and later spread across the county. In fact, they fought their hosts and defeated them at Aylesford, a Medway crossing, giving them control of the whole county as far north as the Thames.

But they were not able to take advantage of that conquest without the reinforcement of more European mainlanders, and the people who came to take over the newly won territory were not quite the same as the original Jutes of East Kent. They were near relations but sufficiently different for the two sides of the Medway to make a distinction among themselves, and for that distinction to be inherited, certainly in county lore and for much of the Kentish history, too, by later generations.

So to this day, the River Medway divides East and West Kent, and if the distinctions between the Kentish Men and the Men of Kent is no longer as marked as it must once have been, still they cling to the conviction that it exists, and take pride in the fact that no native of the county can be neither one nor the other.

Much of the lore of the Thames and Medway rivers has grown up around the people and the boats that have used them as major commercial highways ever since men first went afloat on these islands.

The Thames and Medway barges evolved as specialist craft, and the men who sailed them were specialists, too. Until the end of the eighteenth century, barge traffic tended to be limited almost entirely to the rivers and the estuary, but after about 1860 they began to venture further afield. A golden age for barges dawned just before the mid-1860s, after which the picturesque workhorses of the waterways spread their wings and began to make epic journeys. Their skippers became their own lore-makers.

Carrying cargoes of between a hundred and two hundred tons for the most part (although some later carried more) and crewed by two or three (seldom as many as four) – one of whom was likely to be the skipper's wife – they became familiar all round the English coast. Some sailed to the Scottish islands, to Ireland, and many of them were as familiar with the inland waterways of Europe as with those of the British Isles.

They crossed the Channel and the North Sea, and some of them even battened down their hatches and butted through the Biscay gales with as much phlegmatic imperturbability as if they had been nosing up some east-coast creek.

Bargemen used to boast that they could take their really rather remarkable craft anywhere at all after a heavy dew. They did draw incredibly little water, even when loaded so heavily that the deck was scarcely above the water level.

There is one wholly loreful story told by Frank Carr in his book *Sailing Barges* of a barge mate who fell overboard while the barge was crossing Maplin Sands off the Essex coast. The captain was below, and the mate was the only crewman on deck – until he quitted it unintentionally. The barge sailed on without him over water so shallow that he was able to run after it, splashing through the water behind the boat.

Another story from the same source illustrates the normally very localized experience of many of the old barge skippers. It tells of a London river barge which took aboard a cargo for Margate, although the skipper had never been below the Nore before and didn't know the way. So before he sailed, he asked directions of a coasting-barge colleague. Then, following instructions, he sailed down the Thames into the estuary, crossed the Swale and 'turned right', following the shore line.

But the weather thickened, and it was hazy by the time he approached Herne Bay. Unfortunately, the coasting-barge skipper who had directed him had reckoned without the habit of river barges of staying close inshore and had not thought it necessary to mention Herne Bay pier as a landmark, so when the stranger to those parts saw the pier looming ahead of him through the mist, he intoned a brief incantation that must have made his colleague's ears burn, quickly lowered the mast and shot under the pier, never doubting that it was a bridge he had not been told to look out for.

It used to be a familiar sight to see barges apparently crossing dry land under full sail in many of the coastal marshland areas of Kent. The land is so flat in places that a barge navigating one of the many creeks and tidal waterways looked as though it were gliding over the surface of the land. For anyone not used to it and who did not know the geography of the locality, it was an uncanny sight.

Largely because of this ability to make way over incredibly shallow water – but also partly because it was perfectly true! – barges earned a reputation for smuggling and sheep-stealing. It used to be said that many a sheep on the North Kent marshes hobbled about on three legs because a barge crew had had the fourth for a Sunday dinner! Lies, all lies – as every barge crew that worked those parts would have told you.

Smuggling was different, though. It was not unknown for barges to be built with secret compartments and hollowed-out beams specially to carry illicit cargoes, usually trans-shipped out at sea from ocean-going vessels. Many stories are told of the ways in which the barges supplemented their legitimate cargoes with better-paying ones brought in right under the noses of the Customs inspectors.

In the days when barges sailed with hay piled so high on the deck that they looked like waterborne haystacks, such a deck cargo was a perfect hiding-place, and although officialdom was not unaware of what was going on, it simply was not practical to search every barge any more than it would be to search every lorry today.

The barges built up a significant body of lore around themselves during both twentieth-century world wars. They continued trading all through the First World War, and a great rivalry grew up between them and the Royal Navy, which was responsible for all shipping, because, the barge men claimed, the Navy men did not understand sail and sometimes made impossible demands upon the sailors, who were wholly dependent upon wind and tide and with the best will in the world could not obey some of the regulations that officialdom tried to impose on them.

Often, of course, there was not the best will in the world between the two anyway. The barge crews were contemptuous of Naval officers' lack of understanding and love of red tape, whereas the Navy regarded the barge men as insubordinate and irresponsible.

During the First World War many of the barge mates were still the wives of skippers, and one of them, Mrs Charlotte Whale of Strood in Kent, claimed to be the only woman entitled to wear a Mercantile Marine medal. She earned the distinction by volunteering to sail as a barge mate in 1914 and had a number of eventful voyages. She survived several life-threatening adventures only to be wounded by shrapnel during the very last Zeppelin raid of the war.

Barges were among the 'little ships' that sailed to Dunkirk in 1940, and they featured in other wartime roles, too. They were almost uniquely suited to work that necessitated navigation through seas sown with magnetic mines, because their wooden hulls meant they were far less likely to fall victim to such weapons than the more usual metal vessels.

There are some barges still left today, although they cannot compete as trading vessels with the road-freight vehicles. There is still an annual barge race, successor of the series of races initiated by Mr Henry Dodd in 1863 which gave birth to a few legends of their own. During the heyday of the barges, many were built primarily to win the annual races, and some of them became legends themselves. One of the most famous of the Medway barges was *Giralda*, which won many races.

For centuries Gravesend has been the port of entry of London's river. Ships bound in for the Port of London called first at Gravesend, and vessels leaving England made Gravesend their last call before heading out into the open sea. The very name of the town is what is left to us of the Saxon Gerevesend, indicating the limit of the Portgereve's (later Portreeve's) authority.

In 1866 Gravesend offered a grandstand view of the beginning of the final stage of the most incredible race of any by the legendary China tea-clippers. Of sixteen clippers that left Foochow Harbour laden with tea for London that year, the race for home soon singled out four ships to be remembered for a hundred years for their performances: *Ariel*, *Fiery Cross*, *Taeping* and *Serica*. The four battled it out all the way; sometimes one was in the lead; sometimes another. For much of the way, they were within sight of each other, and they all crossed the Equator on the same day.

By the time *Taeping*'s steam tug hauled her into Gravesend, almost an hour before *Ariel*, both vessels had to wait there together for the tide to turn. The tension was enormous, for there were big money prizes to be won by the crew of the first vessel to dock in London, and this was the closest race ever recorded, with only the length of the River Thames left to cover.

The two clippers left Gravesend practically side by side on that last dash upstream. In fact, *Ariel* arrived outside East India Dock gates at nine o'clock in the evening. *Taeping* did not reach London Docks, further up river, until 10 p.m. But this almost unbelievable race was still being timed even then, because *Taeping* actually docked first. Drawing less water, she was able to go through the lock and finally docked just twenty minutes ahead of *Ariel*.

That was the closest finish to any China tea-clipper race before or after that date, and it was finally agreed that the bonus of ten shillings a ton for the cargo should be awarded to *Taeping* but shared equally with *Ariel*. It was, in fact, the last time a bonus was offered for the first cargo of tea to be brought by the China clippers to London.

The £100 prize for the winning ship's captain was presented to Captain MacKinnon of *Taeping*, and that, too, was halved with *Ariel*'s Captain Keay.

Gravesend was also famous for its ferry, which was certainly of great antiquity and was probably unofficial before it was granted to the town to help raise money for repairs after Gravesend was sacked by the French in 1380. The right to operate the Long Ferry, as it was called, was kept by Gravesend for more than four hundred years. It was a cheap and comfortable alternative to a long overland route into Kent to travel from London by the Long

Ferry to Gravesend, there to disembark and travel across country to destinations in Kent.

It was not, however, altogether safe, and fatal accidents were tragically commonplace. The ferry developed its own distinctive kind of vessel, known as a tilt boat, which had an awning under which passengers were protected from some of the worst weather.

As well as having the Long Ferry, Gravesend was also one terminal for the Cross Ferry – indeed, it still is, though precariously, as economics drive its owners, British Rail, ever nearer to threatened closure. It operates from Gravesend to Tilbury and back again and is the oldest river ferry in south-east England. It probably began as a right exercised by the Manors of Tilbury and Parrock (Gravesend), but in 1540 it was taken over by the garrison of Tilbury Fort.

There is a legend that Charles I used the Cross Ferry in 1623 when he was Prince of Wales, accompanied by the Duke of Buckingham, on his way to woo the Infanta of Spain. The story goes that the Duke gave the ferryman a gold piece for the fare, which was so much more than the usual that the ferryman suspected they were either spies or gentlemen travelling to fight a duel. He had his two passengers arrested.

Gravesend corporation acquired the ferry rights with the Manor of Parrock in 1694, and in 1851 took over the sole rights of the ferry in both directions. They leased it to private operators, including railway companies, which is how it passed to British Rail, who withdrew the vehicular ferry in 1964 and now operate only a foot-passenger service.

There used to be ferries across the Thames from Deptford, Greenwich, Isle of Dogs and Woolwich as well as from Gravesend. The Woolwich ferry claimed to be a royal ferry and in 1330 petitioned Parliament to suppress its rivals at Greenwich and Erith simply because of its royal patronage.

The first free ferry – Woolwich Free Ferry – was opened by Lord Rosebery, chairman of the London County Council, in 1887, amid scenes of great rejoicing, with streets decorated and lined with soldiers for the procession. The ferry came to be used as a day's outing in itself for Londoners, who used to take picnics aboard and enjoy the 'cruise'.

The ferry earned its place in history during the Second World War when, in 1940, it spent one whole blitz-blazed night evacuating people from Silvertown on the Essex side to the comparative safety of the Kent bank, through a curtain of blazing oil that had quite literally set the Thames on fire.

The Thames has always been a busy river, and, almost inevitably, much of the lore of the river has its origins in tragedy. The worst of those was that which befell the *Princess Alice* pleasure paddle-steamer in September 1878.

She was returning from Sheerness and Gravesend to London with more than nine hundred passengers aboard. Many of them were women and children, returning from a day out in the famous Rosherville Gardens at Northfleet, just along the river from Gravesend. It was a popular outing venue for Victorian Londoners; there was a bear-pit, an aviary, a zoo and botanical gardens, a maze, tea-rooms and side-shows. In the evenings, there were illuminations, dances and balls and two theatres, one of them open-air.

The *Princess Alice* had left the Rosherville Pier and was steaming upstream at 6.10 p.m., with an irregular helmsman who had taken over from the usual crewman. The band was playing and passengers were dancing, and there was a generally festive air aboard. Few of the passengers saw the collier *Bywell Castle* bearing down on them off Woolwich, in a stretch of the river known as Gallion's Reach or, sometimes, the Devil's Elbow.

What happened is pretty well established. Why it happened even the inquest failed to find with any real certainty. What is certain is that the *Bywell Castle*, a much bigger vessel than the little paddle-steamer, hit the *Princess Alice* amidships, just forward of the starboard paddle-box. The smitten vessel simply folded in the middle and began to sink at once.

Six hundred and forty men, women and children were drowned in that one tragedy, and 240 children were orphaned. Woolwich Town Hall was made into a temporary morgue for the bodies that were recovered by dozens of small craft that put out from both banks.

The inquest was held in Woolwich Town Hall, and a long-drawn-out and rather bitter affair it was. The crews of both ships blamed the other, and the whole nasty business ended with a squabble among the jurymen, who were locked in all night in an effort to reach a verdict, when four of them, including the foreman, were so opposed to the majority view that they refused to sign the necessary papers. It was exactly the sort of situation that lore thrives upon, and the whole tragic incident has become embedded in the lore of the Thames.

It was not, of course, the only tragedy to mar the history of Britain's busiest and most historic waterway. But it was the worst. The collison between the steamer *Oriole* and the liner *Corinthian* off Greenwich in 1914 was no less tragic for those who died, although the death roll was not nearly as long as that of the *Princess Alice*. It might have been worse if the ferry *Golden Eagle* had made it a three-vessel collision, as it nearly did, but neither history nor lore has a lot of time for might-have-beens.

No doubt there was a great deal of lore attached to the infamous prison hulks which festered among the Thames and Medway mudbanks during the early part of the nineteenth century, but little of it seems to have survived as, indeed, few of the prisoners consigned to them did.

Dickens added his own contribution to what lore remains when he wrote *Great Expectations* and gave Pip his dramatic encounter with the escaped prisoner Magwitch. That, of course, was fiction. The facts were of convicts, hulked for very minor offences, crowded together, more than a thousand of them, men, women and (comparative) children to each hulk.

The hulks themselves were the hulls of old wooden vessels, pensioned off and moored among the estuarial mudflats to become rotting, waterlogged prisons afloat. Escape attempts were rewarded with severe floggings, and disease and illness among the convicts ended more sentences than time-served releases did.

The bodies of those who died aboard the hulks were rowed ashore and buried in unmarked graves on the marshes, where, a century later, they were still struggling to the surface to disconcert less barbaric generations of finders of human bones. One of those burial places, off Hoo Peninsula opposite Queenborough on the Isle of Sheppey, is still, today, called Deadman's Island.

The hulks began as temporary accommodation for French prisoners of war but continued in use for civilian prisoners after the defeated soldiers had gone home again. They were overflow prisons from the great prison camps that were established in different parts of the country and from the castles and public buildings that were pressed into service for the purpose. Word of conditions aboard the hulks got around, and it was said that the threat of imprisonment in them did a great deal more than their own officers did to stiffen the resolve in battle of French soldiers.

At one time there were more than sixty of these hulks all filled to overflowing with men so wretched in their captivity that, manacled and leg-chained though they were, they faced almost certain death in the foul water or evil-smelling oozes rather than remain aboard. If they were seen escaping, they were likely to be shot – a fate many of them must have felt was infinitely preferable to the living hell of the hulks.

For the people who lived by or near the river, the prison hulks offered an occasional alternative to the more commonplace smuggling in which many of them engaged. Prisoners who were able to contact friends or sympathizers who could raise the necessary money could – and did – bribe their way to freedom, with the bought help of the local people.

Men familiar with the creeks and channels of the lower Thames and Medway could organize help for convicts once they were clear of the hulks, picking them out of the water at prearranged points or taking them aboard from points around the coast, according to what escape plans they had been able to negotiate. Then the local men slipped across the Channel to Continental ports with their human cargoes and not infrequently made the return trip with a few cases of brandy or Brussels lace aboard, just to make quite sure the risks they took were worth their while.

There is a tale of one occasion when one of the vessels, having arrived to rendezvous with its latest escapee found the man still chained to the rest of the gang. All the men had to be taken as a job lot, so to speak, but they could not be off-loaded for onward trans-shipment until they had got rid of their encumbering irons. So the men were put ashore near Whitstable and left to make their own arrangements for the rest of the journey home. The story does not tell how many of them – if any – made it to the other side of the Channel, but it is said that, when a house in Whitstable was pulled down some fifty years ago, more than two hundredweight of rusty iron manacles were found under the floor.

The local men found the business of trading in escaping prisoners so profitable that they organized highly efficient escape routes and systems, very similar in operation to those which became familar to many escaping British prisoners of war in France during the Second World War. Remote houses and farms were used as 'safe' hide-outs where the escapees could stay in relative security until money had changed hands and arrangements could be made for their sea voyage to the Continental mainland.

One of the once remote and little-used lanes near Whitstable that were used for this traffic used to be called Cut Throat Lane – it is now known as Pilgrims Lane – but the old name had probably clung to it from a time long before the nineteenth-century hulks began to put money in the local pockets and almost certainly had no direct bearing on a business that, nevertheless, had a certain very literal cut-throat element about it sometimes.

The most famous of a number of escape agents was a man who was known to his contacts in Whitstable as James Moore but who could very easily have hid his identity under the famous Scarlet Pimpernel symbol. He was a somewhat dashing young man who seemed to have plenty of money, who spoke French as well as he spoke English, and was well-known to lie equally well in both languages.

Where he came from originally remains something of a mystery which he himself never seems to have made any effort to clear up, but he arrived in Whitstable and bought a well-known local hoy that was already notorious for previous owners' smuggling activities. He specialized in meeting escaped prisoners in London and bringing them down the Thames and round the coast to Seasalter, at that time a very sparsely populated coastal village next to Whitstable, which itself was no great town at that time. There he trans-shipped them to another boat of his, called *Two Sisters*, in which the escaped prisoners were taken to the Continent. Most of Moore's work must have been done more with bribery than with any real derring-do because his activities seem to have been less than securely cloaked in secrecy.

One of his clients was a particularly important prisoner, a French general, who travelled with another important escapee. They took a roundabout route that finally brought them not to the Kent coast but to Hastings, where, after staying in hiding for some time, they were arrested as they emerged to take ship for France. Moore, using the name of Harman at that time, was arrested in a notorious smugglers' inn some way out of town and sent to jail. After trial, he was 'sentenced' to service with the Navy.

It wasn't very long before he found himself aboard the Nore guardship *Namur*, where he very quickly used the escape organization he himself had set up and was soon safely back in Whitstable. His business had been carried on in his absence, and he married a local girl.

Some time later, after another arrest, Moore returned to the escape business in Scotland. He was again jailed, and quite what happened to him after that neither history nor lore seems inclined to tell us.

Two other loreful tales of the Thames demand to be told before we turn to other Kent waterways. They are both true but both very much of the stuff that lore is made of.

In 1620 a well-known waterman of his time, John Taylor, bet some of his friends that he and another man could sail a paper boat from the City to Queenborough on the Isle of Sheppey. The wager attracted a lot of attention and brought out thousands of people to line the river banks on the day that the feat was due to be performed. Many of them, no doubt, thought that the whole thing was a hoax and that the attempt would not be made, but they still wanted to be there – just in case.

In fact, Taylor and his friend made their paper boat and launched it and set off downstream in it. Within half an hour the boat had begun to fall apart, but the two men in it had equipped themselves with bullocks' bladders which, when inflated, served as lifebelts.

Thus buoyed up and with the soggy remnants of their paper craft clinging to them, they did, in fact, reach Queenborough, where they were greeted by the mayor and generally made much of while the local people tore off whatever they could of the shreds of sodden paper and boat to keep as souvenirs. It was reported that many of them stuck bits of the mess in their hats to signify that they had been among those present on that memorable day. The wager was won, though not, perhaps, quite in the spirit in which it was made.

More than 250 years later, in 1875, another bit of Thames lore was bequeathed to posterity by fourteen-year-old Ann Beckworth when she swam the five miles from London Bridge to Greenwich in one hour and eight minutes.

Lurking off Sheerness, waiting to burst its way into history and, no doubt, give rise to future lore in the event, is the wreck of the American munitions ship *Richard Montgomery*. It has been there ever since it ran aground in 1944, loaded with high-explosive bombs – more than three thousand tons of them.

It is quite visible, particularly at low tide, and the people of Sheerness have been uncomfortably aware that, if ever it was struck by another ship, there could be a truly devastating explosion that would certainly do a great deal of damage to the town. Officialdom recognizes the danger, and periodic checks are carried out to judge whether the risk has increased. So far, the verdict has always been that it is less hazardous to all concerned to let the *Richard Montgomery* lie with her cargo intact than to try to tamper with it or take it off.

Some experts say the danger gets less as time goes by and the effects of sea water reduce rather than increase the likelihood of an explosion, spontaneous or induced. Others are equally sure that the danger is as great as ever it was and forecast that, sure as anything, one day the ship will blow up. But even they cannot predict with quite what force that will happen, forty years after the bombs were packed with their high explosives.

Of the other Kent rivers, the River Limen is something of a legend on its own. Today there is no River Limen, but in Saxon times and before that it flowed into the sea somewhere near Hythe. It was, in fact, the Limen into which the Danish army sailed with 250 ships in 893, the year the Danes built a fort at Appledore and wintered over ready to go into their burning, pillaging and raping routine with unusual thoroughness right throughout the south-east of England the following year.

The Limen formed a northern arm of the River Rother which ran into a kind of delta of tidal swamps beyond the Isles of Ebony and Oxney and past Appledore. But in 1287 one of a series of unprecedentedly severe storms changed the course of the river so that it took a shorter route south to join the sea at Rye, across the county boundary in Sussex.

After the change of course, the delta silted up and added good acres to the Romney Marsh, once they were drained, and the River Limen was no more. Today the Rother is wholly in Sussex except for a short stretch where it is shared with Kent as part of the county boundary. The old River Limen is remembered only by place-names such as Port Lympne, the beautiful old mansion (the grounds of which are a private zoo) deep inland and high on the still clearly discernible shoreline that overlooks the flatness of Romney Marsh spread out below it.

Nearby Lympne Castle reminds the twentieth century that it was once necessary to fortify this ancient shoreline, and below the present castle the remnant ruins of so-called Stutfall Castle recall the days when Romans knew this coastline – now several miles inland – very well.

In East Kent now the river is the Stour, which rises in the southern slopes of the North Downs and flows down to Ashford, where it joins the little East Stour and turns sharply north to become the Great Stour. It flows through Canterbury and joins the Wantsum, the once-navigable channel that cut off the Isle of Thanet (but is now little more than a ditch and barely discernible even as that in places). Near the junction, the Great Stour is joined by the Little Stour, and the combined waters turn east to cross Ash Level and meet the sea at Sandwich.

In doing so it flows through the ancient and tiny borough of Fordwich, which was once the port for Canterbury. It was at Fordwich that Caen stone from France was landed to be carried to Canterbury for the building of the cathedral. It was to Fordwich, too, that came the shipments of wine for the monks of the abbey.

Fordwich was one of the early limbs of the Cinque Port of Sandwich and had its own mayor and jurats and the right to punish its own criminals by drowning them in the river.

The Canterbury and Whitstable railway ended its days as Canterbury's port – a position usurped by Whitstable after 1830, although there was still a quay at Fordwich in 1893.

Today the town is a picturesque waterside resort, the town badge incorporating a trout on a plate. It is that crest that earns it a mention among a collection of Kentish lore, for we have it on no less authority than that of the great fisherman Izaak Walton himself that this was once the home of the Fordidge trout; a trout, he wrote, 'that bears the name of the town where it is normally caught, that is accounted the rarest of fish; many of them near the bigness of a Salmon'. He went on to say that, despite the reputation of the town for its Fordidge trout, none was known to have been caught by an angler there – 'except possibly by Sir George Hastings, an excellent angler, and now with God'.

Certainly the singular trout, that rarest of fish, is no longer to be hooked out of the River Stour at Fordwich, and only the words of old Izaak and the plate of trout on the town arms remain now to allow this pretty little river to burble its way into Kentish lore.

10

The Lore of Industry

It is not easy to picture the scene now amid the quiet rurality of the Weald of Kent, but once this was one of the most important centres of industrial England, equivalent to the Black Country today. The great Wealden forest provided what must have seemed at the time like inexhaustible supplies of wood, for both the machinery of the age and the fuel that served it. There were, too, a great many small streams coming down from the High Weald watershed which could be harnessed for water power, and, of course, there was iron.

Iron was already being worked in the Weald before the Romans came. Not very efficiently, by later standards, but in some quantity, nevertheless. The 'bloomeries' in which the iron was extracted from the ore were large kilns which produced rather a lot of impure slag which was virtually waste material as far as the iron-masters were concerned. The Romans recognized its value in road-building, and one of the ways in which modern archaeologists have been able to identify Roman roads through iron-working areas, including the Weald, is by discovering the slag along the old routes.

Later, particularly after the Flemish weavers were encouraged to settle in England, when many came to the Weald, it was the cloth industry that flourished, alongside the iron furnaces, though not usually in precisely the same places.

When seventeenth-century conservationists, whose concern was not, as is that of their contemporary counterparts, for ecological balance so much as for defence of the realm, began to win their arguments for not clearing the forest to extinction, both iron and wool had to look elsewhere for their prosperity. It was the emergence of coal as the fuel of the future that shifted the heavy industry away from the south of England to the Midlands and the North, and the Weald slid gently into the same sort of dependence upon farming that most of the rest of the county had had for centuries.

At the beginning of the nineteenth century, Kent was almost wholly agricultural. The dockyards at Chatham and Sheerness were the largest industrial centres, although there were fairly small-scale paper-making industries dotted around the county, notably at Maidstone, Crayford, Eynsford and Buckland and in the Canterbury area.

At that time Whitstable had its oysters and a fairly minor source of local pocket money in copperas which was extracted from a particular kind of pebble found locally on the Whitstable and Isle of Sheppey beaches and used in dyeing and tanning, but otherwise most of the coastal areas depended heavily upon fishing and smuggling.

There was some boat-building, brewing, brick- and tile-making, chalk and stone-quarrying, and salt was produced at Stonar near Sandwich, on the Isle of Grain and at one or two other places. But none of these was of more than minor local importance economically. The main wealth of Kent was in the land, and it was controlled by the men who owned the land, who, in turn, depended upon the men who worked it.

The first of the large-scale modern industries to come to Kent was cement-making, and that was followed by the development and to some extent the concentration in the north-west of paper-making. It was not until the end of the century that a lucky strike by men sinking the first shaft for the proposed first Channel tunnel confirmed geologists' predictions that there was coal in East Kent and began an oddly alien mining industry there.

All industry engenders its own lore. Inevitably, then, with such diversity of industry over the years, a great deal of lore built up in each section. Much of it remains untapped outside the circle of people involved with the particular industry. But much is available for its collectors, still. For instance, to begin at the beginning with iron, Kent had two of the most renowned foundries in England, at Horsmonden, which specialized in casting cannonballs for the army, and at Lamberhurst, where the famous Gloucester Furnace was.

It was the Lamberhurst ironworks that made the iron railings for St Paul's Cathedral in London, but it also made large numbers of cannons, some of which were smuggled out to French vessels during the wars with France. That sort of thing could not, of course, be allowed to pass unpunished, and the town of Lamberhurst was heavily fined for allowing it to happen.

During the seventeenth century, Tonbridge (then Tunbridge) was recognized as a source of particularly fine cutlery. Later it became possible to talk of Tonbridge as the Sheffield of the south, but, of course, in its heyday no such comparison was possible.

Cloth-making was a widespread cottage industry long before the Flemish weavers arrived in Kent during the fourteenth century. What the 'strangers' brought with them was a new talent for making very much better and finer cloth than the English cottagers had been making until then.

The newcomers favoured the Weald of Kent for several reasons, but among them were the availability of their raw material, wool, from the Romney Marsh flocks, the suitability of the local water for washing the cloth, and the convenient proximity of fullers' earth in the Maidstone area. The fact that they were near the sea and the shortest sea routes to the principal export markets of the day was no disadvantage, either.

The woollen cloth-making industry of the Weald of Kent has probably left the county more scraps of lore than any of the others. The characteristic Kentish grey colour of the cloth that came to be so closely identified with the region left its mark on the name that lingered even after the industry itself had declined: Kentish Greycoats. It was a name that stood for solid worth; for those yeoman qualities that were so admired – and so coveted, in some cases – by others all over England.

Cranbrook became the heart and centre of the Wealden cloth industry, the only town in the Weald that can be said to have developed wholly as a result of industrial rather than agricultural interests. It became a very prosperous town, and there was a hint of ostentatious prosperity in the gesture with which the people of Cranbrook welcomed Queen Elizabeth I to the town during her progress through Kent in 1573. They laid a mile-long path of local broadcloth for her to walk on.

It was wool, too, that created the much romanticized fraternity of Owlers, the Romney Marsh smugglers who specialized in breaking the trading laws of the sixteenth and seventeenth centuries by shipping wool straight from the farms to foreign weavers. According to the tradition, well established in fiction but with little enough support elsewhere, they earned their name by their practice of signalling with imitations of the cries of owls as they picked their way across the ditch-scarred Marsh at night.

In fact, although wool was for centuries the staple commodity underpinning the basically agricultural economy of Kent, East Kent (and particularly the Canterbury area) was at one time equally famous for its silk weaving. A memorial of the old industry is still to be found in the city centre, beside the River Stour in the much-visited Weavers. The old building still invites tourists to its upper floor to see the old looms.

It was Queen Elizabeth I who offered sanctuary in England to French Walloons from the religious persecutions in their own country, and the Canterbury Burghmote records show that in 1577 the foreign weavers were granted an allowance towards the maintenance of their trade halls and were allowed to use the crypt of Canterbury Cathedral to store their looms and other materials while they settled into new homes in and around the city.

Working under articles granted by the mayor and magistrates of Canterbury, the Walloons were permitted to make boys' clothes and cloth 'after the Flanders fashion'. A hall was found for them in the Friars, where their goods could be displayed and examined, and they were allowed to take their products to London and elsewhere to sell them, too.

But in a world where nothing is given free, the Walloons had to pay for the privilege of having their cloths officially approved. Later, too, they had to pay a loom tax. In abut 1582 there were 390 taxed looms in Canterbury; by the early seventeenth century there were more than a thousand silk-looms at work there. But native craftsmen protested and petitioned, and finally the Walloons were forbidden to compete with English weavers. That meant they had to develop new and distinctive products that did not compete. Naturally, high prices could be demanded for such products, so the immigrants probably did quite well out of their hosts' constraints. The Canterbury silk-weavers were soon selling directly to the very highest of London society, including royalty.

After the silk-weaving industry wilted under pressure from much cheaper Oriental imports towards the end of the eighteenth century, a certain John Callaway gave it a new direction by inventing a process for making Canterbury muslin, but the decline continued.

That much is properly history. More loreful is the story of two Canterbury ladies who, at the end of the nineteenth century, decided to resurrect the virtually dead weaving industry in Canterbury. They took the trouble to learn all they could about silk weaving from experts in London and Bradford and then set up three looms in the Weavers at Canterbury, where they employed other workers to help them.

The story of the brave attempt to revive the Canterbury industry is true, but it is equally very much of the stuff of legends.

The two ladies, fired with an almost crusading zeal, persuaded the City charity trustees to find apprentices for them, and, eagerly passing on their own so recently acquired skills, they proceeded to weave brocade. The first piece that came off the new looms was presented to the Princess of Wales (later to be HM Queen Mary, grandmother of the present Queen). It was worn by her during the celebrations for the coronation of Edward VII.

Sadly, as is the way of legends so very often, the high hopes faded, this time under the assaults of contemporary commercial competition. The resuscitated industry suffered a relapse and, despite all the efforts of its two patronesses, died.

Ah well, there's no gainsaying the lore loves a tragedy. It really is astonishing how many legends depend for their being remembered at all upon the tragic element that runs through them.

The history and lore of Kent's gunpowder industry certainly include a full measure of tragedy. Kent claims to have been the county in which the British gunpowder industry began. Its birthplace was the town and creekside port of Faversham, whose first historian, Edward Jacob, claimed that the first gunpowder works in the town were established in the reign of Queen Elizabeth I, if not before her time, even.

Certainly the town was ideally suited for the industry: easy access by water, near to the sea and the ports of the Thames and Medway, where the chief markets were, and within easy reach of the charcoal that was a major ingredient of early gunpowder.

In fact, gunpowder was made of saltpetre, charcoal and sulphur. Both the saltpetre and the sulphur had to be imported, which was another good reason for establishing the gunpowder works near the sea and near to docks where the importing ships could deliver it. Water was needed to power the mills that ground and mixed the ingredients under pressure, and at Faversham the stream that fed the creek was perfectly suited to the work.

After that first mill was opened at Faversham, several others followed. Throughout the early days, certainly, and probably for much of its history, gunpowder was handled by the local smugglers as readily as any of the more well-known commodities like

St Edith's Well at Kemsing recalls the tenth-century birthplace of the daughter of Edgar, first King of All England

The detached belfry of St Augustine's Church at Brookland, Romney Marsh, is said to have fallen off the church in surprise at evidence of local morality

The Devil's Kneading Trough at Wye has a serenity that belies its place among Kent's profane lore

The soaring defences of Dover Castle have challenged the lore makers down the centuries

The distinctive white-framed, round-topped Dering windows
at Pluckley are particularly well illustrated at the local inn

Rochester Castle—does the beautiful Lady Blanche, accidentally killed by her lover's arrow, still haunt the historic ruins?

Lympne Castle, on the edge of the old Romney shoreline, has the much-haunted look that local lore claims it deserves

Cooling Castle, on the North Kent coast, is said to be haunted by one-time owner Sir John Oldcastle

Lurking lore? Second World War munitions ship *Richard Montgomery*, believed by some to be destined to devastate the Sheppey shoreline some day

The East Kent hooden horse may be a relic of Saxon rituals of two thousand years ago

Restoration House at Rochester was written into Kentish lore by
Charles Dickens

Broadstairs, on the Isle of Thanet, still takes very seriously its
associations with Charles Dickens and keeps alive his characters during
the annual Dickens Festival

Bleak House at Broadstairs is the starting-point of all the local Dickensian lore

Before the TIR juggernauts had to be re-routed round Canterbury by the bypass, local lore had fun with tales of demands for the Westgate Towers to be pulled down to let large vehicles through

Reculver Towers—sometimes called 'The Brothers' in memory of the de Birchington twins, Father Richard and Sir Robert

wool and silks, laces and tobacco. The powder was smuggled out of the mills in small and sometimes even quite large quantities and shipped abroad or to foreign vessels out at sea.

One of the privately owned mills at Faversham was taken over by the Government in 1760 to become the first Royal Gunpowder Factory in the country, although, of course, there were other powder-mills elsewhere in Kent and in other parts of the country, too.

Explosions were accepted as an inevitable hazard of gunpowder manufacture. The makers provided for them and designed buildings in such a way that the least possible damage was done, and that of a kind that could be quickly repaired. Jacob explained how the millhouses were made of only lightly fastened fir boards, so that, when 'by accidents, no way to be accounted for, they blow up', the lack of resistance meant that very little real damage was done, although he also acknowledged that sometimes the damage was much greater. The damage to workers was, apparently, of less consequence, for he made no mention of that, beyond saying that, 'In this hazardous employ there is never a want of hands, light labour and constant pay are two strong inducements easily prevailing over the fear of danger, especially as the labourers are certain of proper care taken of them in all misfortunes.'

So the history of the gunpowder industry in Faversham, as elsewhere, is scarred with a series of explosions of varying seriousness. In 1767 one damaged ancient Davington Priory, and in 1781 a much worse one did a lot of damage to part of the town, where one house was completely blown down and the noise of the explosion was heard in London. The flames were seen in Thanet. Yet in that particular explosion only three men were killed.

It was after that that a new factory was built outside the town on the nearby marshes, and it was there, after its invention in 1846, that guncotton was made. Guncotton was much more powerful than gunpowder, and Faversham was certainly the first place where it was manufactured. Production started in 1847, and only some six months later there was a disastrous explosion in which twenty people were killed. The mill was a mile outside the town, yet in Faversham itself people cowered from the explosion which broke windows and uprooted trees.

That explosion brought to a halt the manufacture of guncotton for a while, and the mill went back to making gunpowder instead.

But gunpowder was going out of fashion now. A few years later, guncotton was again being made in Faversham, this time using a new and improved formula. There were still accidents, though on a smaller scale, until the town's worst explosion rocked Faversham in April 1916.

Then, more than a hundred employees were killed by a TNT explosion. It was the sort of tragedy in which legend revels, and long after the explosives factories had gone from Faversham, people remembered the Big Explosion and the mass funeral of the victims at the town's cemetery.

Today gunpowder mills at Faversham are a tourist attraction – though, of course, they no longer mill gunpowder. The Chart Mill on the creek's headwater stream has been expertly restored to working order and can be visited for demonstrations of how the work was carried out. It is, in fact, the only survivor of its kind in the United Kingdom now, which brings the town full circle in the gunpowder-manufacturing industry's history: from first pioneer to last survivor.

When gunpowder was being introduced to the workforce of Faversham, further west along the Kent coast at Dartford a German immigrant called Spielman was setting up his mill, the second paper-making mill in England. Curiously enough, that mill was later converted for gunpowder manufacture.

It was French refugees – the same wave that brought silk to Canterbury – who brought paper-making skills to England, and by the end of the seventeenth century there were several mills in Kent, including a small one at Aylesford where now there is the international giant Reed paper-mill.

Maidstone became one of many paper-making towns in Kent. The River Medway, as well as its tributaries, provided the water needed both in the manufacturing process itself and for powering the machinery that was used in it. In fact, it was at Maidstone, in one of the many mills that had, for centuries, been powered by the little River Len, that the famous Turkey Mill brand was produced two hundred years ago. It became recognized as one of the industrial wonders of Europe and producer of some of the finest paper of its kind in the world.

The mill itself was an old one, certainly predating 1640, when it was known as Overloppe Mill, and in 1657 it was one of many fulling-mills in this part of Kent. By the time it was converted to paper-making in 1694, it was already known as Turkey Mill, and it was under that famous name that it continued to make paper until 1976, when it went into liquidation.

Paper-making succeeded iron and wool as one of the few staple industries of Kent. Another was cement-making, which is still important today, particularly in the north-west, where it has helped to shape the countryside with its vast pits and excavations from which the raw materials of the industry are won.

The lore of the industry has given to a man called Aspdin the role of father of the industry. It was he who, in 1824, patented Portland Cement, a name he borrowed from an earlier pioneer, John Smeaton, who used a mixture of clay and lime and Italian volcanic materials to reproduce a cement with some of the under-water hardening qualities of ancient Roman cements.

Smeaton used his cement for his Eddystone Lighthouse in 1756 and claimed that it equalled the best Portland stone in solidity and durability. The same cement was used by Isambard Kingdom Brunel for his famous tunnel under the Thames in 1838, but the first true Portland cement was produced in quantity in about 1845 at Swanscombe by firing a mix of chalk and clay at high temperature. A block of this concrete was shown at the Great Exhibition in London in 1851 as one of the wonders of the age.

Since then, cement-making has established itself in the Swanscombe, Dartford and Gravesend area and boasts one of the largest factories of its kind in the world at Northfleet. Cement has been made for a very long time on the banks of the River Medway, too, notably at Halling, which can be said to have been brought into existence, certainly as it is today, by the industry.

Unfortunately, a great deal of industry in Kent has flourished only by gouging out great holes in the county's surface. Agricultural lime-burning has, for centuries, bitten deeply in the North Downs chalk, but on an insignificant scale compared with the gaping scars left by cement-making, the sand and gravel extractors, brick-makers and, most recently, coal-miners.

Geologists had long predicted that there would be coal under parts of East Kent before Francis Brady carried out his test-boring for the first Channel tunnel excavation in 1882. The coal was discovered by accident by the tunnellers, but it was soon being exploited and has added significantly to the county's industry ever since, even though the Channel tunnels on-and-off record continues yet.

But however much individual industries have contributed over the centuries to Kent's history and lore, nothing, perhaps, has had more historic and loreful impact upon the county than the railways. Kent boasts the first passenger railway, the longest straight stretch of railway in England, the most famous of the little railways and the first standard-gauge railway line to be built under the Light Railways Act of 1896.

In the 1970s it was through Kent that the new high-speed railway linking London with the proposed Channel tunnel was intended to be built, and that became the most highly controversial stretch of railway ever planned in this country. So controversial, in fact, that public opposition to it certainly contributed very considerably to – and some would say it was wholly responsible for – the British Government's decision not to go ahead with the tunnel scheme in 1975.

The first passenger-carrying train service in the world was the Canterbury and Whitstable (affectionately known locally as the Crab and Winkle Line) opened in May 1830. It was that line which moved Canterbury's access to the sea from Fordwich, downstream along the Stour, to Whitstable and which changed the little fishing village into a modern port and harbour.

When it began, to the sound of cannons fired from the city's Westgate Towers and peals of bells from the cathedral, the passenger coaches were pulled, for some of the distance, by the steam locomotive *Invicta*, built by George Stephenson himself in 1825 and still preserved for public viewing in the city.

Because of the very steep gradients over which the line had to run, winding-gear was installed on Tyler Hill and elsewhere to help trains 'over the hump' by pulling them with stout ropes.

It was never an altogether satisfactory service. *Invicta* was the nineteenth locomotive built by George Stephenson at Newcastle, and it ran over the flat stretch into Whitstable for eight years, after which it was taken out of service and replaced by more powerful and more reliable engines. In 1846 the line was taken over by the South Eastern Railway, and after that it was operated by locomotives only over the whole route.

During the years of intense rivalry between the South Eastern and the London Chatham and Dover Railways, the old Canterbury and Whitstable began to lose business after the LC & DR opened its Faversham-Whitstable line in 1860. It lost more when the East Kent Bus Company began to open up its services during the 1920s.

By 1930 passenger services on the line came to an end, and although it struggled on as a goods-only route, that too ended in 1952, and today there is little more than the world's oldest railway tunnel at Tyler Hill to remember it by.

Once it became clear that railway locomotion was rather more than a nine days' wonder, and that there were big profits to be made from carrying goods and passengers by this new means of rapid transportation, railway mania gripped the nation. Railways were built in all directions, and one of the earliest was the eastern part of the Reading-Tonbridge line which opened in May 1842. It was extended to Headcorn later that same year and then went on to Ashford and Folkestone, reaching the sea in June 1843. An extension to Dover was opened in 1844.

The Redhill-Ashford length included the longest straight stretch of railway line in England, a distinction it has preserved until today, and for thirty years it carried Top People to and from the Continent.

The Folkestone-Dover extension was a major feat of engineering involving building a hundred-foot-high viaduct, four tunnels and a sea wall, as well as blasting away part of the famous White Cliffs. But when it was done, it meant that people could travel from London to the French and Belgian coasts or back again in a comfortable single day's journey.

It was not only people in a hurry who valued the service, either. For years, until 1848, both *The Times* and the *Herald* London newspapers retained an SER engine, kept constantly available with steam up, at Folkestone to carry dispatches from the Continent to their editorial desks in London the moment they arrived. Sometimes the two engines raced each other for the distinction of being the first to bring the same news to their papers' readers.

Railway lore in Kent would probably not be as rich as it is if it had not been for the rivalry that sprang up between the South Eastern Railway and the East Kent Railway, later the London Chatham and Dover. The SER monopoly was broken by the EKR first with a line from Strood to Canterbury via Chatham, Sittingbourne and Faversham. From there it spread out: Canterbury-Dover 1861; Faversham-Whitstable 1860; on to Herne Bay 1861; to Margate and Ramsgate 1863; Rochester-Sutton at Hone (now Swanley) and St Mary Cray 1861.

Part of the rivalry between the two companies arose from the EKR's originally advertised role as a local feeder into the SER network in Kent, but the newcomer soon outgrew that modesty and set about carving out its own empire. A whole series of local railways were built, financed for the most part by local men, and they joined together to create the London Chatham and Dover Railway in 1859.

The new company took over one of the Channel packet lines and was then able to compete with the SER for Continental traffic as well. Kent had two routes to Europe by rail.

It has always been a feature of industry that it attracted men away from the land, and the railways were no exception. Some of them built up some of their lore around the characters who drove their trains. One such man was 'Farmer' George Diplock of Paddock Wood, who became an engineman in one of SER's most famous locos. He was noted for getting the best out of his engine, and the sort of lore that outlived him was such as that tale of the time he covered the 88 miles from Dover to Cannon Street in London in 108 minutes, travelling at such high speed through the little station at Staplehurst village that all the station lamps were blown out! What a memorial for a railwayman!

As always, railway accidents make up a large body of the lore of the lines. There was the fortunately more amusing than tragic incident on New Year's Day 1850 when one train ran into the back of another, an empty one, at Gravesend. The empty train ran away, unmanned, and the station superintendent with great presence of mind commandeered an engine and set off in pursuit. He finally caught up with the runaway near New Cross, where, it seems, he performed a daring leap from the cab of his own engine into that of the unmanned one and brought it to a halt in time to avert a collision.

Then, in 1885, there was the ill-fated excursion train travelling from Charing Cross to Gravesend. It gave its trippers more excitement than they paid for, first by running over a donkey and causing a delay while the carcase was disentangled from under the engine's firebox, and then by charging straight at a balloon which had landed on the track ahead of it at Northfleet. The landing left no time for the train driver to anything more than utter a foul oath or a pious prayer (the lore can be tantalizingly imprecise about such details). Whichever it was, it worked, because a gust of wind lifted up the balloon again just in time and set it back down at the side of the track.

Probably the most famous accident of them all in Kent happened in June 1865 near Staplehurst. The train was returning from France to London, and at that time such trains travelled according to when the tides and the winds permitted the cross-Channel ferries to arrive at Kent ports' terminals. On this particular occasion, repair work was in progress to track crossing a bridge between Staplehurst and Headcorn, and a ganger on the line to warn trains of the hazard confused his working schedule and the train's timetable for the day and gave the train the all-clear signal although the line was, in fact, up on the bridge.

He realized his mistake too late. The engine, tender and first carriage jumped the forty-three-foot gap in the rails, but the middle eight coaches crumpled up and crashed over the bridge into the river and swampy fields below.

Unluckily for him, but luckily for us (because the crash would almost certainly have been less well remembered otherwise), one of the passengers in the first of the derailed coaches was none other than the already famous Mr Charles Dickens. Travelling with him was an old lady and his young mistress, Ellen Ternan, with whom he had been on holiday in Paris. Their coach caught on part of the broken bridge and hung there. According to the story that circulated afterwards, Dickens calmed the ladies, climbed out of the window and obtained the carriage key from the guard. He then rescued the ladies and turned from them to tend the injured and dying.

In all sixteen people died in the accident, and some fifty were injured. Dickens and his lady were lucky to escape with nothing more than shock, although it was said afterwards that the novelist never fully recovered from the experience, and there were those who recognized a tragic significance in the fact that he died on the anniversary of the crash five years later, in 1870.

Kent's railways provided the setting for one of the most spectacular train robberies, too. That was in 1855, the same year that Samuel Smiles (he of the Self Help philosophy) became Secretary of the South Eastern Railway – although neither history nor lore draws any conclusions from the coincidence.

What happened was that £20,000 in gold travelling by night mail from London Bridge to Paris just disappeared. It was a complete mystery and might never have been solved had not the leader of the gang that accomplished the deed had a girl friend who worked in the refreshment room at Tunbridge Wells station.

Shortly after the train robbery, he was arrested on a totally unconnected charge of forgery, and he got word to his associates asking them to look after his lady friend until he was free again and could share his part of the gold with her. However, he was imprisoned for the forgery, and while serving his sentence he learned that she was not being looked after as he had asked. Embittered, he turned queen's evidence about the bullion robbery and told the whole story of how it had been planned and carried out.

According to that story a man called Agar, formerly a clerk at London Bridge station, joined another called Burgess (the bullion train guard) and a third called Lester (a clerk at Folkestone station), and together they arranged to get hold of a duplicate key for each of the iron safes in which the bullion was to travel by train. Agar then hid himself in the bullion van at London Bridge and, on the way down to Redhill, put some of the gold in a grip belonging to Lester, which Lester had had locked away in the guard's van as passenger's luggage.

Having taken out the gold, Agar replaced it with the equivalent weight in lead (taken from Lester's bag). Lester left the train at Redhill, claimed his bag from the guard's van and went back to London.

More bags were filled with gold on the way to Folkestone, where the bullion safes were transferred to packet steamer, apparently intact. Agar and Burgess both travelled on to Dover, where they reclaimed their own bags from the guard's van and, weighted down with gold instead of the lead with which they had started their journey, returned to London.

It might well have been the perfect crime, if it had not been for the concern of one man for his girlfriend.

The little Elham Valley Railway was never more than a small local line and no sort of a competitor of the two Kent railway giants. But it shouldered its way into railway lore after a Mr Edward Bannister Callow became company secretary in 1865 and, two years later, absconded with a large sum of company money which he had embezzled. That, too, might well have been yet another unsolved crime if Mr Callow had not got himself into further trouble and ended up in prison in London, enabling the long arm of the law to reach out and pin the Elham Valley crime on him, too.

The company disintegrated after that, and finally there was a Board of Trade inquiry and the company was dissolved, in 1947.

But that was not until after the war had catapulted the railway into national importance if not (because of censorship) notoriety by bringing three heavy guns to use the line to hurl shells into and across the Channel. One of the guns was the famous Boch Buster, its eighteen-inch barrel making it the largest gun of its kind in Europe. It was, in fact, a relic of the First World War, when it had completely destroyed one French railway station.

Throughout the duration of the Second World War it was fired only three times, which was just as well because it was quite capable of doing almost as much damage in the vicinity of its discharge as it would have done to the enemy. It weighed 250 tons and fired shells almost 7 feet long, each weighing 1¼ tons. The first time it was fired in 1941, although nearby villagers were warned to open all their doors and windows, there was still a lot of damage caused by the blast.

As has been said in different contexts: with friends like that, who needs enemies?

Probably the most famous railway in Kent is the Romney Hythe and Dymchurch which crosses the Romney Marsh and is well known to all the thousands of tourists who travel on it every year by the affectionate name of 'The Little Railway'.

The railway was the hobby, in the first place, of two racing-driver friends, Captain J. E. P. Howey and Count Zborowski, who shared an enthusiasm for miniature railways. Together they looked for somewhere to build a railway that would enable them to enjoy their hobby but which would be useful in a wider sense, too. It happened that the people of Romney Marsh were agitating at the time (mid-1920s) for better transport, and the Southern Railway suggested to the two men that here might be as good a place as any for them to put their plans into operation.

Unhappily, Count Louis Zborowski was killed in a racing accident in Italy in what was to have been his last race before he retired to 'play' railways in Kent, but Captain Howey decided to go ahead and work began on the Hythe-New Romney fifteen-inch gauge section of the railway in 1926. It cost about £2,000 a mile to build, and by the end of the year the Duke of York (later King George VI) was able to drive the engine *Northern Chief* along it, although it was not opened to the public until July 1927.

The 5½-mile extension to Dungeness lighthouse was opened in 1929. The Little Railway is very much a part of Kent lore now. During the Second World War, like many of its bigger brothers, it was pressed into national service and saw action with the anti-aircraft train that used its lines. Later in the war, it carried tons of steel pipes and dozens of technicians to help build the equally loreful Pipeline Under the Ocean (PLUTO) which helped fuel the D-day-plus invasion forces.

The railway was reopened after the war in two parts: Hythe-New Romney in 1947 and the Dungeness extension in 1947, when two silent screen and early talkies stars, Laurel and Hardy, drove the engine.

11

Lore Galore

Many of the legends and traditions of Kent can be more or less neatly slotted into fairly obvious categories, but there is lore galore that is much less conveniently categorized and, perhaps for that very reason, less often remembered.

What label, for instance, could be put on the extraordinary tale of the Folkestone Fiery Serpent? The story was first set down by an anonymous eighteenth-century writer, and no one is quite sure if it was an original bit of tongue-in-cheek micky-taking or if it only recorded a much older morsel of mythology. It is a fact that there has been, since time out of mind (as the legal historians put it rather expressively if not very precisely), an element of friendly rivalry between the neighbouring ports of Dover and Folkestone, and the poem, original or not, illustrates that very well.

The thirty verses tell of a strange creature that appeared in Folkestone one day and settled in a field of wheat, from where its eerie screams during the night roused the townsfolk to send out their mayor and jurats to capture it.

Well, the mayor and jurats, assisted by such townsfolk as could best be spared for such a hazardous undertaking, tried all sorts of things. They tried netting the creature, but it flew over their nets. They tried rolling a man in a barrel up the hill to shoot at the monster through the bung-hole, but the barrel rolled down the hill again before it came within gunshot range, and came so near to drowning the man inside by bouncing over the cliff and into the sea that they decided not to try that again.

The vicar told them the visitation was a divine punishment for irregular churchgoing, which brought the people of Folkestone back to church all right, but unfortunately the creature's screeching interrupted the services, so they lapsed back into their old ways again.

In the end, someone suggested that the only way to exorcize this serpent that had come among them was to set fire to the corn and burn it out. Such a serious step, however, deserved the best counsel they could get, and so they sent for the advice of the Mayor of Dover who, together with the entire Corporation of Dover, duly journeyed to Folkestone. After a number of other suggestions had been discarded, they all finally circled the field, guns at the ready, and began to close in on the baleful creature.

Unhappily, when they neared the middle of the field, they all sighted their quarry at the same time, all fired at it together and then, as one man, turned and fled for their lives.

By the time a few of the townsmen had summoned up enough courage between them to return to see what had been the effect of the volley, they found the creature irrefutably dead. But, just to be on the safe side, one man threw a fishing-net over it, and another put a barrel over it, and then they ran back to tell the Mayors of their success.

The Mayors argued over who should be first to peep through the barrel bung-hole at the cause of all the trouble – neither wanting to usurp the precedence of the other! – but finally the honour fell to the Mayor of Dover, whose superior perspicacity enabled him to identify the cause of all the trouble as – a peacock.

About the only thing we can say with certainty about this fun-poking doggerel is that it was written by a Dover man! With whatever authenticity, the incident is now undeniably a fragment of Kentish lore, though I fancy it is rather better known in Dover than it is in Folkestone, and probably hardly known at all anywhere else.

Pseudonymity rather than anonymity veiled, though lightly, the authorship of the *Ingoldsby Legends* which enshrine a number of Kent's most abidingly loreful legends. Purporting to be tales handed down through the fictitious Ingoldsby family and recorded by a member of that family, Thomas Ingoldsby, they are in fact the work of the Reverend Richard Barham, who was born in Canterbury in 1788, became curate at Ashford and later served other Kent parishes, including some of those on Romney Marsh, where he made a hobby of collecting local tales told to him by his parishioners.

He took an appointment as a minor canon in St Paul's Cathedral in London, the better to be able to pursue the literary life, and he used his collection of old Kentish tales as a foundation for the *Ingoldsby Legends* which he published in parts from 1837 until 1845.

The Legends are written in rollicking rhyme that faithfully

reflects their author's basic gentleness and sense of fun, and very entertaining they are, too.

The story of Ellen Cook has already been told (Spirits of the Lore). Another, entitled simply 'The Ghost', might have found a place alongside that one, except that the title is part of the joke of the whole thing. It tells of a poor Canterbury cobbler called Nicholas Mason who was married to a woman 'of a temper somewhat warm'. When roused, she was apparently in the habit of picking up 'a stick or stool, or anything that round did lie, and baste her lord and master most confoundedly'.

Well, one night, the cobbler had a nightmare in which he was visited by a ghost who showed him a treasure vault in old Canterbury Castle. Before the cobbler could reach the hoard, though, he had to dig, and it being (in his dream as well as in fact) dead of night and he with no candle to light his labour, he decided to mark the spot and return to it in daylight. So he reached for his awl and plunged it into the wall – or, rather, into a part of his bed-sharing wife that caused her 'ever from that hour . . . to use a cushion in her chair!'.

'The Smuggler's Leap' is another Ingoldsby Legend, this one centring round an old chalkpit near the village of Acol on the Isle of Thanet, known locally as Smuggler's Leap. The legend, certainly older than Ingoldsby, tells how a certain Sandwich riding officer, Anthony Gill, pursued one Smuggler Bill through a foggy night to the edge of the chalkpit over which they fell together. The twist in the tale was that, although Smuggler Bill and Exciseman Gill were found lying together at the bottom of the pit, only one horse was found with them, and it is said that the site has been haunted ever since by the exciseman's faithful dun stallion.

Although most of the Legends are in verse, some are not, and one of those is the Isle of Sheppey story of Grey Dolphin. This is the story of how the surly Sir Robert de Shurland, thirteenth-century Baron of Shurland and Minster and Lord of Sheppey, killed a friar and was besieged in his castle by an outraged Sheriff of Canterbury and his men, until the knight sallied out and, single-handed, with only his great sword Tickletoby to aid him, routed the lot.

Well, that was too much, and the Pope himself ordered that Baron Shurland should be taken and executed. Easier said than done, though, for this was one of those recurring periods in English history when Pope and monarch were at odds, and the

Baron reckoned that if he could get his King's pardon, he could, so to speak, cock a snook at the Pope.

So, when King Edward (the First, nicknamed Longshanks) sailed down the Thames to review his troops before they sailed off to the French wars, Baron de Shurland mounted his horse, Grey Dolphin, and urged it out into the river, where he made the horse swim three times round the King's ship to attract the royal attention. Then he promised the King that he would serve him in France if he were given a royal pardon for his high-handed homicide. The King, impressed with the style of this knight, and probably needing every such man he could get to join his expeditionary force, agreed, whereupon the Baron tucked the royal pardon safely in his vest (so the Ingoldsby Legend solemnly assures us) and turned his horse back to dry land.

Ashore again, he was met by a mysterious old woman who told him that his horse, although it had saved his life that day, would nevertheless cause his death. More cautious than grateful, Sir Robert did no more than unsheath his sword (the redoubtable Tickletoby, you will remember) and with a single blow cut off the head of the exhausted animal where it stood.

And that, no doubt thought the Baron, was that. But, of course, he didn't know then that he was being cast in the lead role of a legend which, like all legends, did not have to play fair with everyday logic. Sure enough, three years later, while walking on the beach, Sir Robert stumbled across the whitened skull of a horse. Recalling the old woman's warning, he disdainfully kicked the relic back into the water, but as he did so one of the teeth in the jaw of the skull pierced his boot and stuck in his toe, where it festered and, exactly as forecast, caused his death.

The Isle of Sheppey has always been a place of mystery to mainlanders. Even today there is something oddly 'foreign' about it. For its size it has a rather extraordinarily many-faceted character, with the Sheerness docks and industry and the compact domesticity of Queenborough – so named, incidentally, by Edward III, who built a castle there and named the royal borough which he thus established after his queen; the brash holiday camps of Leysdown, the melancholy crumbling clay cliffs around Minster (once near the centre of the island) and the remote marshlands of Elmley.

The island may well have the longest history of human settlement of anywhere in Kent, and it is said by some to have been the last remote stronghold of the old druidical rites in England, long after the Romans had left, when Saxons and Danes warred for mastery of the county and the country.

Perhaps the Old Ways were still practised, a little furtively, out there on the Elmley marshes, even while the seventh-century Princess of Kent, Sexburgha, and her nuns performed their own early Christian rites in the Minster she built and which survived the determined vandalism of Danish raiders and Saxon rebels alike, only to be destroyed as a result of Henry VIII's dissolution of the monasteries, leaving just the church and the old minster gatehouse for modern visitors to see.

We know very little now of druidical practices, but rather more about Saxon customs, many of which linger, if only in vestigial form, in everyday Kentish life.

Hoodening may be one such. Many people believe that this Kentish oddity, which once seemed to be dead but which was revived and is now very much alive again, is a direct descendant of a Saxon celebration connected with their veneration of horses.

The hooden horse was once an almost universal feature of Christmas in East Kent, where farm labourers, and particularly wagoners, brought it out and went a-hoodening from house to house, collecting (almost demanding with menaces, indeed) money for their own festivities.

The Hoodeners always included the Wagoner with his long whip, the Horse (a man under a sacking 'body' concealing the stick to which was fixed a wooden horse's head with a hinged jaw worked by a string), the Rider, who tried all the time and always hilariously unsuccessfully to mount the horse, and Mollie, a man in 'drag', who went behind the horse sweeping vigorously with a besom broom. With them went two or three musicians, according to what local talent and musical instruments were available.

The Wagoner would lead the capering Horse from door to door, where householders would be summoned to face viciously snapping wooden jaws, often studded with hobnails to represent teeth, until they contributed money, cakes and ale, or some other appeasement to send the Hoodeners on their way.

Sometimes the real head of a dead horse was used instead of the wooden replica.

The name Hoodening derives from the Hooden or Hoden Horse, and many a loreman will tell you confidently enough that the name is a corruption of the original Saxon Woden's (or Odin's) Horse.

There is a story that the practice was banned in Thanet during the first half of the nineteenth century after the Horse scared a woman to death. Certainly the hoodening had become an excuse for serious rowdyism and licence by then, but it was still going strong, though not necessarily in Thanet, in the 1860s.

There is a story that a Hooden Horse so frightened another lady, who had been an invalid and unable to walk for seven years, that she jumped out of her wheelchair and ran indoors – and was able to walk perfectly well for the rest of her life.

The Morris, which sometimes incorporates a hooden horse, is not, however, the same as hoodening. The Morris is common to many parts of Britain, with local differences, and today Morris teams often include traditions from other parts of the country in their own repertoires. No doubt Kent had its own peculiar Morris rituals, but although there are several Morris teams dancing in Kent today, it is by no means always easy to disentangle traditional Kentish dances from those borrowed from elsewhere. The Morris, therefore, while loreful enough, is not specially Kentish and need delay us no longer.

An Easter custom once apparently unique to Kent was that of Pudding-pieing (or, if it really was unique to Kent, pudden-pie'n, as it would certainly have been called). Pudding-pies were traditionally part of the Easter and Lenten fare: round and flat, usually about the size of a tea saucer, although some were larger, with a raised crust filled with custard and with currants sprinkled on top. As well as being eaten in the home, pudding-pies were also expected to be on the bill of fare at public houses, where they were commonly washed down with another local oddity, cherry beer.

A Kent custom that was certainly current during the eighteenth century and was probably very old then was associated with Shrovetide, when in villages and small towns all over the county the boys and the girls gathered in their own groups at opposite ends of the main street or in otherwise well-separated parts of the town. The boys had an effigy which was known as a 'holly boy' and the girls one called the 'ivy girl'.

The ritual began with raids, boys upon girls, girls upon boys, during which the effigies had to be captured or stolen, so that the girls ended up with the holly boy and the boys with the ivy girl.

The effigies were then burned amid noisy acclamations – but nobody seems to know why. There is a theory that it had more to do with St Valentine's Day than, properly, with Shrove Tuesday, although other theorists have wondered if it did not have more to do with ancient harvest home rituals than either of the other two.

Whatever was the origin and purpose, there seems every likelihood that it dated back to pagan times. Holly and ivy were both plants that featured in our pagan ancestors' festivals and may very well have kept alive some long-forgotten and not wholly Christianized festival.

Old Woolwich used to perpetuate a curious St Clement's Day (23 November) custom during which blacksmiths' apprentices processed around the town accompanying one of their seniors disguised behind a mask and wearing a wig and a long white beard and coat in the role of Old Clem. He was seated in a great wooden chair covered with bunting, and he carried a wooden anvil, tongs and hammer, the tools of his trade.

His attendants carried other percussive tools of various kinds: sledgehammers, battleaxes and the like, and there were flaming torches to light the processional route. The procession itself was traditionally headed by a drum and fife and by six men carrying the seated Old Clem on their shoulders. From time to time they would stop, and Old Clem would recite a prepared speech at each stopping-place.

Whether or not this was a Kent tradition rather than a black-smiths' apprentice tradition familiar in other parts of the country too, I really am not sure.

The same is true of the May Day revels during which it was the custom for sweeps to elect one of their number as Jack in the Green and go walk-about through the town. The Jack in the Green custom was certainly not confined to Kent, but whether it was equally traditional elsewhere for the role to be played by one of the town's sweeps I couldn't say. All I know is that the chosen Jack was dressed in a conical wicker framework covered in holly and ivy at the sharp end of which was perched a crown of flowers and ribbons. Other sweeps dressed up too, as clowns, lords, ladies and so on, and danced round the Jack in the Green to the accompaniment of pipe and drum music.

At the village of Old Wives Lees, between Canterbury and Ashford, it became traditional during the seventeenth century, and for some time after that, for two young men and two maids to race each other on 19 May each year. The prize was endowed by Sir Dudley Digges, who left £20 to be paid to the winner of the race, the money to come from the rent of lands in the parish which came to be known as 'the Running Lands'.

There is nothing exclusively Kentish about curious kinds of rent paid for land or other property, but still Kent has had its fair share of some of the most curious. Many of them have long since lapsed or been replaced by more orthodox, if less appealingly loreful, currency.

The Lord of the Manor of Grange (then known as Grenche and now part of Gillingham), for instance, held his land in return for service to the king or, in lieu, presentation to the monarch of a pair of silver oars whenever called upon to meet his obligations.

The Manor of Seaton at Boughton Aluph near Ashford was held in 1232 in return for providing eight greyhounds and a handler for the king whenever he went to Gascony, but the obligation was specifically limited in time for 'as long as a pair of shoes of fourpence price should last'.

At Wilmington, land was held from the king in exchange for a single pot-hook for the king's meat 'whenever he should come within the Manor of Boughton Aluph'.

Three maple cups presented at Edward III's coronation were the rent for land at Bilsington on the edge of Romney Marsh, and later, in the reign of Charles II, the tenant had the extra duty imposed upon him of carrying the last dish of the second course to the King's table.

Just outside Dover were once manors whose tenants held them on condition that, whenever called upon to do so, they should accompany the monarch on cross-Channel voyages with a silver bowl at the ready in case of a touch of the royal *mal-de-mer en route*.

One substantial volume of lore is bequeathed to us by each generation of authors exercising their skill at making fiction mimic fact so convincingly that the two become confused in the readers' minds. There is a good deal of lore of that kind in Kent, especially in and around the Medway Towns and in Thanet. Charles Dickens left his mark on both areas to such an extent that there is rivalry between the two areas to claim to be the premier shrine of the nineteenth-century writer. Both hold Dickens Week festivals; both have Dickens museums; and local lore is founded upon the great man's sojourns in both places.

In Rochester, tourists are invited to note Restoration House, not so much because of the tradition that Charles II stayed there when he returned to England from foreign exile in 1660 (which he may well have done) as because it contains what is always known as Miss Havisham's room, the room which Dickens borrowed and made the very one in which Pip met the eccentric old lady in *Great Expectations* (which it most certainly was not.)

At nearby Cooling, the churchyard includes a grave marked with thirteen small lozenge-shaped stones which is today only known at all to most people because Dickens made it the family grave of Pip's relations in the same book. At Chalk, near Gravesend, there remains – though barely, for it is in a sad state of decay now – what is widely known as Joe Gargery's Forge, although, of course, Joe Gargery was never anything more than a figment of Dickens' imagination.

At the opposite end of North Kent, in Thanet, Broadstairs harbour boasts that it is overlooked by Bleak House itself, even though the house is no longer as Dickens knew it when he lived there, and many shop fronts and garden gates in and around the town cultivate the local Dickensian connections.

But Dickens is not the only writer to have contributed to county lore. Shakespeare gave us Shakespeare Cliff near Dover, one of the celebrated White Cliffs, so called for its description in *King Lear*.

Chaucer, too, has peopled whole housing estates with memories evoked by the street names of his *Canterbury Tales* characters, and in the picturesque little village of Elham, east of Canterbury, the old Rose and Crown Inn likes to boast that it was once host to the Scarlet Pimpernel himself, Sir Percy Blakeney, the creation of authoress Baroness Orczy.

Down on Romney Marsh you may still have pointed out to you landmarks linked with the likeably infamous Dr Syn, the smuggling cleric immortalized by Russell Thorndike. Indeed, visitors to Dymchurch, scene of so much of Syn's fictional activity, might be lucky enough to arrive during the town's Day of Syn, when the local guardians of the lore are wont to dress and behave in commemorative fashion.

As a matter of fact, Broadstairs could have made quite a local hero of Richard Joy, the so-called Kentish Samson, if it had not got rather carried away by Dickens. Joy lived there in the early eighteenth century and made a name for himself by performing

feats of incredible (an appropriate word!) strength. His fame
spread beyond the county confines and took him to London,
where he performed before William III. His party pieces included
pulling against 'an extraordinarily strong horse' and pulling a
rope capable of taking thirty-five hundredweight. He went in for
lifting enormous stones, too, and generally showed almost as
much imagination in his claims as he did strength in his undoubted displays.

Inevitably, though, the limitations of his particular talents
eventually meant that the novelty of his prowess palled, and he
came back home to Thanet, where he seems to have settled down
to the life of a local smuggler, in pursuit of which career he was
drowned. He was buried in the church of St Peter's at Broadstairs.

Incidentally, while we are still in Thanet, we might take our
leave of it with a nod of acknowledgement in the direction of that
very ancient belief that the name of the former island derives from
a Greek expression of the peculiar quality of the local soil that
made it poisonous to snakes, with the result that no snake could
survive there.

The miscellany of lore is almost inexhaustible. At Boxley, just
outside Maidstone, you may visit a very small stream which runs
under and alongside the road in perpetuation of a loreful conviction that this is none other than that very stream that inspired
Alfred, Lord Tennyson, to write one of his best-remembered
poems, 'The Brook'. Tennyson was a guest at Park House at
Boxley, which was built in 1785 but demolished in 1955, so there
is certainly no special reason why the little waterway should not
have found fame by way of his lordship's inspiration.

Every time we take a picnic, we bite into a little bit of Kentish
lore – even though the Kent connection must be admitted to be a
little strained. It was John Montagu, fourth Earl of Sandwich,
who is said to have invented and given his title to the sandwich
from his combined need to eat and reluctance to stop gambling
for long enough to take a proper meal. Sandwich is, after all, in
Kent – even if the Earl himself very often was not.

Talking of Sandwich, William Lambarde, in his *Perambulation of
Kent* in 1576, gave Sandwich, once Europe's premier port, a claim
in lore to have been founded by a king who, approaching the
Kentish shore from the sea, took it into his head to hurl a hatchet
ashore (for reasons that no doubt seemed perfectly sound to His

Majesty at the time). Where the hatchet landed, the first houses were built in what was to become the town and port of Sandwich.

Interestingly, though not necessarily significantly, of course, there is another story that when, in 1023, King Canute gave the monks of Christ Church, Canterbury, land on either side of the high-tide mark at Sandwich, he stipulated that the extent of the gift should be for 'as far as a man could throw an axe'.

Lingering in this part of Kent for a moment, we can take time to recall the old story of the solitary wayside elm tree that once stood alongside the Dover-Deal highroad. It tells how a soldier garrisoned at Dover Castle killed a comrade with a stick. No one saw the crime, and the murderer was so sure he would get away with it that he stuck the stick into the ground, saying he was safe so long as it did not take root. Soon after that, his regiment went abroad, and it was more than twenty years later that the soldier returned to Dover, to find his stick had, in fact, taken root and was a flourishing young elm. Stricken with remorse, the now old soldier confessed, was tried, condemned and hanged in chains beside the tree.

In Strood and Frindsbury, the memory still lingers of a time when villagers used to go to Rochester Bridge every May Day to fight with the city boys. Most of the latterday combatants had no idea why they did it; it was just one of those time-honoured annual rituals that were too much fun to abandon. But then, as law and order took a tighter grip, the custom died out.

In fact, though, it began as long ago as 1193, when Bishop Glanville of Rochester founded Strood Hospital. The story is told of how the monks of Rochester resisted the building, fearing it would upstage their own Priory of St Andrew, and a feud began between the two interests that lasted for many years.

Once, during the reign of Edward I (1272–1307), at a time of great drought in the area, the monks of Rochester decided to hold a special procession and service in Frindsbury to pray for rain. When the day fixed for the ceremony dawned, a gale was blowing and the monks asked permission to take a short cut through the Strood Hospital grounds. Although the hospital master agreed, many of his brethren did not. So thoroughly did they not agree, in fact, that they hired some local ruffians to stop the procession. When the monks and the ruffians met, there was a fight, and although the procession was broken up, the monks apparently acquitted themselves pretty well.

The affair caused quite a stir, and there was an official inquiry into how it happened, and the upshot of it all was that, since nobody could or would identify the hirelings who caused the trouble in the first place, the men of Strood and Frindsbury were ordered to expiate their discourtesy by walking, carrying clubs, to Rochester Bridge on Whit Monday every year, and there to hand over the clubs to the Prior in symbolic acknowledgement of their collective guilt.

The ceremony later degenerated into something of a rowdy day out for the local lads. Instead of the clubs being handed over on Rochester Bridge, they were used in the free-for-all that ensued when the city boys met the no-longer penitents. From Whit Monday, the event was moved to the more appropriately licentious May Day, but in the end it had to be stopped.

It is tempting to wonder if a similar kind of contribution to future lore might be the now already traditional clash of rival gangs of youths during Bank Holiday weekends in various Kent coastal resorts, particularly the Thanet port of Margate.

The virtually universal custom of showering bridal couples with confetti or rice and of forming an arch of significant symbols as they leave the church once had a variation which has been claimed to be unusual outside if not actually unique to Kent, and particularly the Weald.

There it was traditional for the church path to be strewn with emblems of the groom's work: so, a carpenter would lead his new bride out of the church porch onto a path strewn with wood shavings; a shoemaker onto a litter of leather parings; a blacksmith through a hazard of old iron scraps.

The tradition died out after it became the habit for unpopularity or disapproval to be demonstrated by the substitution of old cabbage leaves, miscellaneous litter and more offensive rubbish for the emblems. Soon, inevitably, the disrespectful rubbish was more popular, even when it was not intended to be taken at all seriously, than the real thing, and then, of course, it had to be discouraged and gradually it died out altogether.

There is a fairly widespread belief that seeing magpies means different things according to how many are seen together at one time. This has a localized Kent variation which applies the predictions to crows instead of magpies. Thus, to see one crow is, in Kent, a good omen. To see two is even better. Three foretell receipt of a letter, four a funeral.

'Five for silver, six for gold; seven for a secret never to be told!'

In spite of that, though, it is still reckoned to be bad luck to see one crow yourself unless you can attract the attention of someone else to it before it flies away. Then the luck changes from bad to good. That is lore well worth remembering when you take a walk with a Kentish countryman, because then you will not be puzzled by his apparent conviction that you must want to have every single crow he happens to see pointed out to you.

One phenomenon which has become particularly associated with Kent is the annual cross-Channel swim, although the swimmers themselves certainly do not come only from Kent. In fact, they arrive from all over the world to try to set up new speed or endurance records in the busiest seaway in the world, or merely to prove to themselves and the world that they can swim it.

That all started in August 1875, when the now famous Captain Webb swam the Channel for the first time – at least officially. For long before that, way back in the days when England and France were at war, and French prisoners were held in various parts of Kent, including the infamous Medway hulks, it was rumoured that some of the prisoners of war escaped by swimming home. There seems to have been no proof that any did, although certainly some tried. On the whole, the likelihood is that none ever succeeded in reaching his homeland in that way. Channel swimming is a feat of endurance that demands peak fitness and a certain amount of preparation if not *in situ* training, and it can be said with some certainty that any Napoleonic prisoners of war who got as far as starting such a swim were very unlikely indeed to have been fit enough to finish it.

But the stories are resurrected from time to time and, to be fair, where no proof that they are true is to be found, neither is any proof that they are not, which makes them legitimate local lore.

No miscellany of Kentish lore would be complete without at least a mention of three quite different but very persistent stories of different vintages.

In chronological order, the first dates way back to 1211, when it was first reported that a mysterious 'ship in the clouds' dropped anchor in a Gravesend churchyard. This improbable story was made even more improbable by the detail that a man 'swam' down the anchor cable to try to free it, but could not, so the cable was cut and the ship sailed on. As though they were not enough, the story went on to assert that a local blacksmith used the abandoned anchor to make ornaments for the church lectern from its metal.

It's a story that crops up in all the best collections of UFO (unidentified flying objects) reports, but its curiosity value is rather enhanced, if anything, by the fact that, to the best of anyone's knowledge now, no one had coined the UFO label in 1211, so that, if the story was not true, it was a fairly remarkable bit of imaginative minstrelsy. Yet how could it have been true?

Then there was the fabled circus that could not get its wagons through the famous Westgate of Canterbury. The Westgate Towers are today one of the old city's proudest landmarks – and one of its worst bottlenecks. The whole city has been bypassed now, and what traffic must go through the gates is not seriously inconvenienced by having to do so in single file. But time was when those towers seemed almost like two great vertical rollers, squeezing the traffic flow like steel ingots going through the mill and coming out reinforcing-rods.

The story the locals love to tell is of how once (the date is never altogether precise, but it seems it may have been at the beginning of the present century or late in the last) a travelling circus came to town, intending to set up its attractions in fields on the outskirts of the town. The procession of wagons with the animals in them arrived at the Westgate Towers and passed through – all of them, until the great elephant cages tried it. They stuck between the towers and seemed all set to stay there.

The circus owner sent for the Mayor, who came and looked and sent for the Corporation, who all came and looked and sent for the police, who confessed they didn't know what to do. But the circus owner was a resourceful sort of man, who came up with the obvious solution – pull down the towers. Well, the police didn't think that was on, and consulted the Corporation, who were almost sure it wasn't on, and called back the Mayor. The Mayor said certainly not and refused to budge from that position.

Luckily for the towers – and the elephants, too, no doubt – once the circus staff saw that the obvious solution was to be denied to them, they redoubled their efforts to free the lodged wagons and finally succeeded, so that the Westgate Towers survived to feature in this lovely little bit of local lore to this day.

That, at least, is the story. During the Second World War it was updated, in fact, and the circus owner became the officer in charge of an American Army convoy of heavy lorries anxious to reach the top-secret areas of the South Kent coast, and the elephant trucks became one of the lorries. Otherwise the story is much the same. I am told the locals find that the first story is favourite among Europeans and native English tourists, but that the second, updated, version tends to go down best with American and Japanese visitors to the city. There is probably a lesson in national characters to be learned from that.

No account of Kentish lore would be complete without mention of the Tovil Treacle Mines. The one-time village of Tovil is now completely absorbed by Maidstone, which claims its riverside industries and its paper-making – and the headquarters of the Kent Fire Brigade.

The history of the Tovil Treacle Mines was outlined in a letter to the *Kent Messenger* on notepaper letter headed 'Tovil Treacle Mines Coy Unlimited (Mineralogists), Pioneers of High Grade Syrup, Treacle and other Sticky Products'. The letter went on to apprise readers that the company was founded, as British Treacle Ltd, in 1181 and taken over 'by the present company in 1182'.

'The ore-bearing rock is somewhat similar to that used at coastal resorts (except for the lettering), is brought to the surface in trucks, and crushed at the refinery,' this interesting, not to say unique, account went on, elaborating helpfully: 'It is at this point that the stickiness is added.'

There is an official history of the Tovil Treacle Mines, too, which traces their origins back through the mists of antiquity, possibly having been founded by Phoenicians who carried the treacle back with them to Gilead. That history claims that a very ancient treacle tin bearing unmistakably the letters 'T – T' was unearthed near Kit's Coty, showing that either the Phoenicians or early Romans evidently used the place as a half-way house on their journey to the port of Rochester.

Indeed, the official history asserts that it was the far-flung fame of Tovil treacle that persuaded Hengist and Horsa to settle in Kent about the year AD 450 and that King Alfred (presumably the Great since there has only been one) was very partial to treacle tarts made with Tovil treacle 'for it was whilst he was so engrossed in savouring their wonderful flavour that he unfortunately allowed the others to burn.'

Apparently, it was for the express purpose of being able to control the mines that Canute the Dane invaded England, and William of Normandy landed at Hastings because that was the most direct route from Normandy to Tovil. The prime purpose of the Domesday Survey was, in fact, to make sure that there should be fair shares for all of Tovil treacle.

There is much more, but perhaps I have quoted enough to give the flavour of the seriousness with which Tovil takes its treacle mines.

12

The Best of Kentish Lore

It is generally recognized as good practice to keep the best bits until the end. That applies no less to lore than to anything else, and Kentish lore includes some marvellous stories which might equally be true or wholly legendary but in either event are much too good to deserve anything less than rather special treatment

The following selection is, inevitably, a reflection of a very personal view of the pick of the crop and is offered as nothing but that. Nevertheless, for one reason and another, they are, perhaps, specially representative of the kind of stories that make up the whole body of lore in Kent.

For instance, there is the earthy little story of St Eanswine (sometimes remembered as Eanswide), daughter of Eadswald, King of Kent, who was given land by her father on which to build a nunnery at Folkestone. She performed a number of miracles, but one which is always remembered with special affection in Kent was performed while the nunnery was being built.

The story recalls that a carpenter – and how such a carpenter came to be employed on such a task or, indeed, if he remained in such employ for very long is not part of the tale – cut a length of timber for one of the beams and misjudged his measurement by three feet, so that the beam would not span the space for which it was intended.

Well, even saints and daughters of kings do not like to have to bear the expense of the ineptitude of their employees, so St Eanswine, instead of abandoning the beam and having another cut to replace it, invoked her miracle-working gifts to lengthen the piece of wood so that it fitted exactly into place, and the work of building could go on.

Many a craftsman since must have wished fervently for such a conveniently devout overseer, and there is no doubt that the comparatively modern onset of do-it-yourself might do a lot worse than adopt the Saxon saint for its patron.

Then there was a story left to us by a monk at the great Cluniac abbey which King Stephen built at Faversham. The monk was called Richard of Rochester, and, writing in about 1470, he related an occasion when King Alfred the Great came to Kent to drive the Danes from the county.

It is a specially interesting little tale because the lore of the south-east does not have a lot to say about King Alfred, who is generally reckoned to belong more to the Wessex region, where he features more frequently in legend and lore. In fact, it is impossible to say with any certainty now that the King himself ever did set foot in what is now Kent, although his army certainly did, and, kingship being what it was in those days, it is not unreasonable to suppose that Alfred had to be in evidence, not just commanding his followers to go into battle but also doing his fair share of the fighting with them.

Anyway, Richard of Rochester told the story of how the Danes came up the River Medway, seeking plunder of silver and gold 'and all else that good is' in the Saxon town of Rochester. The monk reminded his listeners, more than six hundred years after the event and no doubt relying upon what must already have been established lore in his home town, that the invaders 'ate your meats and drank your wines, and all drunken used your maidens perforce; your wives also'.

(Anyone who suggests that sex and violence are new ingredients of popular tale-telling, and puts the blame on television or any other dramatic medium, should read a few of the stories told by the most respectable lore-mongers of centuries past. There is no doubt that among the best remembered of them are those in which the sex is most violent and the violence most sexy – which certainly says more about the taste of the audiences than the licentiousness of the story-tellers through all the ages.)

Richard of Rochester summed up the situation rather well, perhaps, with his declaration: 'O woe the sad Tymes, When man colde not save ne his House ne his Horse!'

But the Danes were halted in their rampage along the banks of the Medway when they reached the fortress city of Rochester, where they were held off while word was carried to Alfred, who at once began a march to raise the siege of the town. When news of the Saxon relief reached the Danes, according to the Faversham monk long after the event, they decided that discretion was the better part of valour. They had apparently heard that, when

Alfred unleashed Saxon fury on plunderers of all that is good and drunken users of maidens perforce – and wives also – heads and other odds and ends were apt to fly. They decided that, if there was any flying to do, it had better be done while they were still intact.

As Richard of Rochester himself described their reaction: 'Fly, Alfrede that Devil is coming,' they said, and they left their loot and their dead and ran back to their ships, fearing 'your good King more than God or the Devil'.

To be sure, Wessex could not hope to be able to keep such a king to itself.

We noticed that St Bartholomew's Day battle off Sandwich in 1217 (Chapter Seven, War Lore) but omitted a lesser-known aspect of the lore connected with that historic occasion because it had less to do with war than such a chapter heading demanded and also because it is, undoubtedly, one of the more spectacular legends of Kent and so is, perhaps, more appropriately included here.

The leader of the French force that sailed for England that St Bartholomew's Day, Eustace the Monk, was reckoned by his followers to be endowed with supernatural powers. When he gathered his little armada together, he had promised his men that there would be no real problem about landing and settling in that green and pleasant land across the Channel, and so confident were many of them that they had brought their wives and babies with them, all ready to start into settling here as soon as their feet were dry after wading ashore.

They saw no reason to approach England with any special caution. They simply sailed for Sandwich, the best nearest port, and the Portsmen of Kent watched them coming and knew they had nothing like the necessary number of ships ready to put up much more than a token resistance. They did what many another despairing defender has done before and since: they fell to their knees and prayed.

They directed their prayers specially to St Bartholomew, it being his day and he being, therefore, the saint most likely to be in a receptive mood. Being worldly wise people who did not expect something for nothing from this world nor the next, they promised that, if they were, despite all probabilities, victorious in the coming clash, they would build a chapel to the saint. Then, feeling no doubt that they couldn't say fairer than that, they got up from their knees and set about the practicalities of preparing for the engagement.

Now the story goes that there was among them in the town a man called Stephen Crabbe, who professed to know Eustace well. Indeed, the two had once been on such terms that Eustace had taught Master Crabbe some of the magic for which he was himself renowned. As a result of this, it was Crabbe who was able to point out to his townsfolk the remarkable fact that, although the French fleet was in plain view, the ship in which sailed its leader, Eustace, was nowhere to be seen. It was, to put it plainly, invisible.

No one else seems to have noticed this, but when attention was drawn to it, of course, it was obvious, and it did nothing to bolster local confidence in the outcome of the encounter upon which they were now about to embark. There were just three ships in Sandwich Harbour at the time ready and able to sail to meet the French, and Crabbe embarked on one of them as they all put to sea.

Well, of course, as already told, the English seamen felt that in the circumstances a certain licence could be taken with the rules of chivalry at sea, and they evened the odds no end by manoeuvring upwind of the incoming French ships and shovelling out quicklime which was blown into the faces of the French seamen, making them easy targets for the Englishmen when they swarmed aboard.

But they had no idea whether or not they were being equally successful against the invisible flagship of the French fleet. For all they knew, Eustace and his shipmates might have been blinded like all the rest, but there is a certain lack of satisfaction in blinding an enemy you can't see. Luckily, they had Stephen Crabbe with them, who alone was able, by the employment of his learned magic, to see the ship in which Eustace sailed. So he had his ship sailed close to where he promised his crew the invisible enemy was, and then leaped over the side of his ship, apparently into empty water. Imagine the surprise of the men left behind on the deck, though, when they saw Crabbe laying about him with his sword, apparently floating in the air a few feet above the surface of the sea.

The fight was a furious one, but Crabbe hacked his way to his chief target and sliced off the head of Eustace the Monk where he stood on the deck of his own invisible ship. As the head left the body, the ship and all the people in it became instantly visible to the English, who no doubt hesitated for a moment or two, nonplussed by all this magic going on before their eyes.

In that moment, one of Eustace's Frenchmen killed Crabbe, and others quickly hacked him to bits and, to emphasize their disaffection, threw the bits overboard into the sea. That might well have turned the tide of the battle, but at that point St Bartholomew evidently felt he had not contributed a great deal so far towards that chapel he had been promised in return for victory.

He caused a great wind to arise, so that all the French ships were capsized, although the English ships were quite unharmed by the big blow. Just to make sure there was no misunderstanding about the indebtedness of the men of Sandwich, as the French ships foundered there appeared in the air a man in red garments who identified himself to the English survivors as St Bartholomew himself, come to help them. Having cleared up that point, he disappeared, and there was nothing for the English sailors to do but turn round and go home.

The people of Sandwich kept their promise to the saint. They built a chapel, and, just to show that they were really grateful, they built some almshouses nearby as well and set aside enough land to support the charity for ever. And, incidentally, to be a perpetual reminder of one of the more bloodthirsty legends – to say nothing of its colourful inventiveness – to be found in the whole body of Kentish lore.

Although, when it comes to inventiveness, you can't do better, very often, than go back to that refreshing fount of county lore, the *Ingoldsby Legends*. We have already dipped into that particular source fairly liberally, but you can't have too much of a good thing. Nevertheless, this must be our last draught, so let's make it a particularly fine vintage, 'The Brothers of Birchington'.

This tale crosses boundaries in that it has elements both sacred and profane and is also an explanation of how a particular landmark came to be named, which could make it a candidate for inclusion among the lore of the land. Instead, and simply because it does combine so many of the loreful elements, here it is.

According to Thomas Ingoldsby (alias Richard Barham), there was once an Austin friar, Father Richard, who was, by popular election of his brothers, head of a priory at Birchington on the Isle of Thanet.

This Richard was everything that a pious monk should have been, and if he had one imperfection it was that he was the twin, in appearances, of his brother, Sir Robert, who, far from being pious, spent all his time in unseemly hilarity and carousing and generally logging up a substantial debit account in the registers of the hereafter. So much so, in fact, that one day the Devil himself, on going through the books, noticed that his Sir Robert was already so heavily indebted to him that he was overdue for foreclosure. As soon as he realized this, Old Nick rubbed his hands together and called one of his imps to him.

'Nip out and collect this knight of Birchington for me, there's a good fellow,' he said. The imp chuckled impishly (how else?) and was just about to set off on his errand when he had a sudden thought.

'How will I know him?' he asked.

Old Nick bent over the books and shrugged.

'We have a description of him here,' he said. 'Unfortunately, through some error, we have him down only as de Birchington, R., but he's about six feet tall, with a little bald patch on the top of his crown – I shouldn't think you could mistake him for anyone else. Off you go, there's a good chap.'

Off went the imp on his mission, not long after the devout Father Richard had left the priory to go to visit his brother, Sir Robert, at nearby Quex Park (Ingoldsby spelled it Quekes, in the fashion of his time and, he averred, the time of the tale, too). When, long after he was expected back by the brothers, he had still not returned, they began to search for him and finally found him dead in a paddock.

Oh, the consternation! The brothers called the mayor and the coroner, and they argued together about who had precedence in dealing with this particular case, and, to shorten a long account, while all the fuss was going on, who should happen along but St Thomas Becket himself.

Well, St Thomas wanted to know what all the furore was about, and when they told him, he blustered and tutted and said he was sure there must have been some mistake because he happened to know for a fact that the good Father Richard's time was not yet come. He thought about it all for a bit and came to the conclusion that this whole business bore all the signs of being an example of the Devil's handiwork. Whereupon he sat about summoning Old

Nick in person to account for his actions insofar as they affected the interrupted longevity of poor old Father Dick.

Thus summoned, the Devil arrived, tail between his legs, and admitted that there had, in very fact, been a mistake. His imp, despatched with instructions only to collect one de Birchington, R., had returned with de Birchington, Father Richard, instead of de Birchington, Sir Robert. As he himself put it (so the legend has it, at least): '. . . somehow – I own it's a very sad job, But – my bailiff grabb'd Dick when he should have nabb'd Bob.'

The saint said that was all very well but he was not going to be satisfied until the error had been righted and that, unless satisfaction was given forthwith to all concerned, there would jolly well be the Devil to pay and someone else to take the reckoning.

Old Nick knew when he was beaten, of course. With a little sigh and a resigned shrug of his shoulders, he agreed to do as the saint demanded. In that instant, the apparently dead Father Richard coughed, sneezed – and lived.

In the very same instant, his brother, Sir Robert, who had been summoned to the scene of the friar's decease, vanished from mortal sight before the very eyes of the assembly. St Thomas was furious. He was having none of that. Although he understood immediately exactly what was going on, he confronted Old Nick once more, arguing that the error had been his and he could not claim twice the same debt. Sir Robert, said St Thomas, must be restored to Father Richard.

Old Nick wasn't happy about it, but he was beginning to be as confused about all these Toms, Dicks and Bobs as you are, and wished he hadn't started this thing in the first place. Petulantly, he flew into a high dudgeon and took himself off, no doubt employing his gift for prevision to sympathize with King Henry II for ranting: 'Who will rid me of this turbulent priest?' As he left, so Sir Robert returned.

St Thomas took the opportunity to lecture the errant knight on the need to mend his ways, and Sir Robert took it all so much to heart that he actually joined his brother in the priory and sold Quex (Quekes) to Sir Nicholas Crispe, whose family, in fact, lived there for several centuries. But the de Birchingtons retained their lands at Reculver on which stood the twin-towered church – and that is how it is that the towers, alike as twins, came to be known as 'The Brothers'.

Because the cathedral of the Archbishop happens to be in

Canterbury, it is inescapable that stories about the incumbent primates have woven themselves into Kentish lore, although, naturally enough, by reason of the office many of the stories are more generally adopted into English rather than merely county lore. However, the story of how Archbishop Sudbury earned himself the fate he eventually suffered at the hands of the peasant rebels in 1381 is quite properly claimed for Kent even though it happened while he was still only Bishop of London and a pilgrim on his way to Canterbury.

On his way he met up with a group of humbler travellers from elsewhere in Kent, whose veneration of St Thomas was characteristically Kentish. He was, for them, the foremost saint in the calendar and to suggest anything less was to invite their righteous wrath. As the travellers journeyed together for a way, the Bishop talked to them about their reasons for going to the shrine at Canterbury. Some of them said they hoped for indulgences from the priests, and the Bishop laughed at them, assuring them that such indulgences were of no value at all.

The pilgrims were aghast at this, to their ears, sacrilege from a man so high in the Church. In fact, one Kentish knight only contained his anger and forebore to draw his sword at the cost of a shouted prediction which legend has preserved for us as: 'Because you have raised such a sedition among the people against St Thomas, at the peril of my soul you shall die a shameful death.' To which the other pilgrims raised a loud: 'Amen!', and the Bishop, who was not particularly adept at what we would today call creating a sympathetic public image, went on, no doubt convinced that you might as well cast pearls before swine as try to teach these Kentish clods anything at all.

The story does not earn a mention in accounts of the Peasants' Revolt by which time Sudbury had become Archbishop of Canterbury in 1375 and Chancellor of England in 1380. Most accounts notice his unpopularity with the rebels and explain it by his office as Chancellor, saying that the peasants blamed him for most of their grievances.

But the story gives a pretty broad hint that the man was far from popular in Kent, at least, among the insurgent counties, long before he assumed that office, and we might wonder if the Archbishop recalled that Kentish knight's prediction on the road to Canterbury as he waited in the chapel of the Tower of London for what had by then become his inevitable end.

He was, it is said, at prayer when the rebels broke in, seized him, beat him and dragged him out to Tower Hill, where they somewhat inexpertly hacked off his head over a log of wood and set it on a pole to be carried in procession through the city to Westminster and back again to join other grisly relics on London Bridge.

Legends do not have to have a moral. If they did, the moral of that one would probably be something to the effect that archbishops should never dismiss too lightly the predictions of Kentish knights they have angered.

Lore and history get pretty close together in the well-known incident of the Civil War that has become known since as the Plum Pudding (some say the Plum Pottage) riots in Canterbury, at Christmas 1647.

Earlier in the year, Parliament had ordained that Christmas festivities in the traditional pattern were illegal, and that included not only all church services on Christmas Day but also the making of plum pottage and nativity pies (which, over the years between, have become Christmas pudding and mince pies). As well, the law required shops to open on that day forbade any decking of doors with traditional holly or other evergreens.

Well, in Canterbury they just were not having that. In outright defiance of the new law, church services were held and shops stayed shut for the day, despite the fact that the Mayor himself went round the town trying to persuade the citizens to obey the law. All he achieved were a few bruises when he was pushed into a gutter.

One thing led very quickly to another. A Puritan supporter shot and killed one of the rioters, the Mayor decided enough was enough and made himself very scarce indeed, and before anyone quite knew what was happening, mob rule held sway in the city and kept hold for several weeks. During that time, the rebels took up whatever arms they could lay hands on – mostly in the pitchfork and mattock line of farm and household hardware – and went on the rampage. They actually broke into homes and demanded to see what Christmas fare there was, and everyone who was found to be without the traditional plum pottage and all the trimmings was lucky if he escaped without being robbed and beaten for a Puritan kill-joy.

'For God and for King Charles!' was their cry (lorefully, if quite unlawfully). 'Plum pottage and sweet Christmas pie!'

But, of course, such joyous lawlessness could not continue indefinitely, even – perhaps especially – during a civil war. Parliament sent a regiment of foot soldiers to Canterbury, and they took down the city gates and solemnly burned them, just for starters.

Everyone who was accused of having taken part in the Christmas rioting was imprisoned, and their leaders and instigators were locked up in Leeds Castle. A special court sat in the city to try the rioters, and a Grand Jury was specially chosen with a view to making sure there was no favouritism. Even so, the jury refused to indict the prisoners, and the trial could not go ahead. The judges were furious about it and kept the accused in custody while the legalities were argued over.

The upshot of it all was that a petition was drawn up for presentation to Parliament. The County Committee (the nearest thing there was to local government at the time) forbade any such presentation and provoked thereby the Men of Kent, fully backed by the Kentish Men, to undisguised insurrection. The whole county was up in arms against Parliament in a very short time. Unluckily – or, not to appear to be partisan in judging history's course, perhaps luckily – the insurgents were not specially well led and no match for the Parliamentary forces when they inevitably arrived under that very able leader Lord General Fairfax.

The rising collapsed after the Battle of Maidstone in which the Kentish rebels were soundly trounced, and although the rumblings of discontent did not subside instantly, the county gradually settled back down and, in fact, virtually dropped out of English history altogether for the next twelve years, until May 1660 when Charles II landed at Dover and began his triumphant and ecstatically welcomed journey to London and his throne.

Ah, slow to anger we may be in Kent; but let any man who tries to stop us enjoying ourselves beware.

But enough of this history-stiffened lore. To return to the real thing, here is an old West Kent story once told as a grim warning to all unfaithful lovers.

It concerns a young Kentish squire who fell in love with his father's maid, a humble brazier's daughter. Despite her protests that she was not his social equal and therefore ought not to listen to his courting, he resolved to marry her, although they both knew that his parents would not welcome such a low-born in-law into the bosom of the family. The young man had an independent income of his own, so he wasn't afraid of being cut off with the proverbial shilling, and in the end he won the girl he had wooed and they were wed, in secret.

It wasn't long before the inevitable happened, and the girl became pregnant. Realizing that, while weddings could be kept secret, pregnancies and their eventual outcome could not, the couple moved to London, but that aroused his parents' curiosity and before long they found out the whole story and caused a great scene.

The expectant father decided that the best thing would be for him to go home and explain and try to win his family round to accepting that what was done was done. So off he went, leaving his wife in London.

He never returned. Instead of persuading his parents to accept his wife, they persuaded him to abandon her. To help him reach his decision, they married him off with almost unseemly haste to an altogether more suitable young woman, and when news of it reached his wife in London, she, poor dear, went into a decline, miscarried and soon afterwards herself died.

A sad enough little cautionary tale, you might suppose. But wait; there is more.

Three nights after her death, her ghost appeared in her former husband's marriage room. Snatching him from his new bride's arms, she claimed him as her own, and, either because he could not resist her or because the experience proved too much for his constitution, he died in her ghostly arms.

As he did so, there appeared on his bared breast these words:

> 'This wretch was my undoing;
> He, being false, has brought me
> To my death and utter ruin.
> For making me his lawful wife,
> The deed he then did smother,
> And for the cursed golden prize,
> He married with another.
> His faithless tongue seduced my soul,
> And easily deceiv'd me.
> His perjured words pierced my heart,
> And of my life bereav'd me.
> Leaving his wife and child to fall
> A sacrifice together,
> He makes a third that caused the ill –
> So now, farewell together.'

No doubt many a young man, warned of what could happen if he allowed himself to fall in love with a social inferior, was asked sternly if he, too, wanted to end up with graffiti of that standard scrawled all over his lifeless breast!

Of course, not only young men are faithless, and there was another story, not all that dissimilar, told to young ladies, especially in the Chatham and Medway Towns area.

That told of a young man of Chatham who courted a girl called Mary Fletcher. Before they were able to wed, however, he went off to sea, but before they parted, the lovers broke a piece of gold, and each kept a piece as a pledge of faith between them.

The young man kept his part of the romantic bargain, but, while he was away, Mary was wooed and won by a farmer's son, and the two were married. When the sea-going swain heard of it, he hanged himself on a tree facing her house where she was sure to see him. Then, to press home the message of his disappointment in her, his ghost paid her a visit in her bed one night and bade her get up and go with him. She did and was never heard of again.

Better men than I have expressed suspicions about another story that belongs to the lore of the Medway Towns. The story was told by William Lambarde, the Kent topographer, in his *Perambulations in Kent* in 1570.

The way he had it, the corpse of a shipwreck victim was washed ashore at Chatham once, long ago, and was buried in the local churchyard, near the shrine of Our Lady of Chatham, which so offended the Lady that one night she left her shrine and went to the house of the parish clerk and woke him up by tapping on his window.

She told him about the offensive burial and complained that this 'sinful person's ghastly grinning' properly upset her. Unless he was removed, she warned, she would be obliged to withdraw her favours from the shrine and stop working miracles among the Chatham worshippers.

Very properly, the clerk felt called upon to take steps to see that this warning did not have to be put into effect. So he took up a shovel and, with the Lady by his side, walked back to the church. On the way, the Lady grew tired and had to sit down to rest for a minute or two by a bush. Where she rested, and indeed the whole length of their journey that night, remained green ever afterwards. (I quote Lambarde, who, of course, foresaw nothing of the intense urbanization of Chatham and the whole Medway Towns area in a future that tended to treat such legends only very lightly indeed.)

After she was rested, the Lady and the clerk went on and dug up the offensive body and took it to the waterside, where it was first found, and cast it again onto the broad back of the River Medway. Appeased, the Lady returned to her shrine, and the clerk went back to bed.

The corpse may well have gone back to sea, only to return with the next tide, and for some time it floated to and fro until the people of neighbouring Gillingham saw it and fished it out. They, too, buried it in their churchyard, whereupon the Rood (holy image of Christ) of Gillingham, which 'a while before was busy in bestowing miracles, was now deprived of all that his former vertue'.

Not only that, but the place where the body was buried continually settled and sank down, and the body could not be disinterred.

Lambarde himself seemed to doubt the motives of the Clerk of Chatham and hinted fairly broadly that perhaps he was not altogether disinterested in the profitable rivalry between the two shrines, at Chatham and Gillingham, and concocted the whole story himself.

Luckily, though, he did not dismiss it so disdainfully until after he had recounted it fully and enriched Kentish lore in doing so.

On that macabre trilogy of witnesses of the richness of Kentish lore I rest my case. Not for a moment do I doubt that every reader who reaches this point will leap up and down in his chair in an uncontrollable passion to point out that I have left out some titbit of tradition, some cache of customs, some latent legend which any fool ought to know about.

No excuses. Lore, like the poor, is always with us, oozing out of every memory that men leave to their descendants. To sweep up every last scrap and fragment of it would be a task such as Hercules, who did not flinch from mucking out the Augean stables, you will recall, would hesitate to attempt.

Remember, Queen Mary, who earned herself the nickname of Bloody Mary for the persecutions that were carried out in her name, took such umbrage at the insurgent Protestantism that inspired the Wyatt-led Kentish Rebellion of 1554 that she swore a solemn oath that she would turn all Kent into a deer park. If she had been able to carry out that threat, she would have acted as midwife to the stillbirth of the last four hundred years of Kentish lore. Indeed, the county turned deer park would have had no need of lore, and all that went before would probably have been lost or forgotten, as well.

Then we might never again have taken pride in such loreful lines as these:

> When order first on earth began,
> Each King was then a husbandman;
> He honoured the plough, and the barley mow,
> Maintained his court from off his farm
> And kept all round him light and warm –
> Like a right good Kentish yeoman!

Index